SABINE LIPPERT'S
BEADWORK EVOLUTION

SABINE LIPPERT'S
BEADWORK EVOLUTION

New Techniques
using
Peyote Stitch
and
Right Angle Weave

LARK

LARK JEWELRY & BEADING

An Imprint of Sterling Publishing
387 Park Avenue South
New York, NY 10016

ISBN 978-1-4547-0824-7

Distributed in Canada by Sterling Publishing
c/o Canadian Manda Group, 165 Dufferin Street
Toronto, Ontario, Canada M6K 3H6
Distributed in the United Kingdom by GMC Distribution Services
Castle Place, 166 High Street, Lewes, East Sussex, England BN7 1XU
Distributed in Australia by Capricorn Link (Australia) Pty. Ltd.
P.O. Box 704, Windsor, NSW 2756, Australia

For information about custom editions, special sales, and premium and corporate purchases, please contact Sterling Special Sales at 800-805-5489 or specialsales@sterlingpublishing.com.

Email academic@larkbooks.com for information about desk and examination copies.
The complete policy can be found at larkcrafts.com.

Every effort has been made to ensure that all the information in this book is accurate. However, due to differing conditions, tools, and individual skills, the publisher cannot be responsible for any injuries, losses, and other damages that may result from the use of the information in this book.

Manufactured in China

2 4 6 8 10 9 7 5 3 1

larkcrafts.com

Credits

Acquisition Editor
Nathalie Mornu

Production Editor
Kevin Kopp

Technical Editor
Claudia Schumann

Art Director
Kathleen Holmes

Art Assitant
Dawn Dillingham

Photographer
Stewart O'Shields

Illustrator
Sabine Lippert

Editorial Assistance
Julie Hale

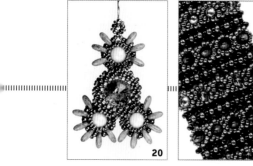
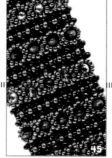
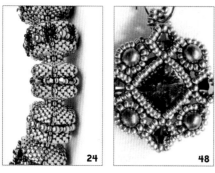

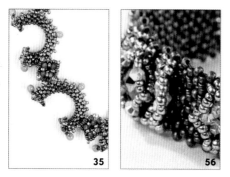

CONTENTS

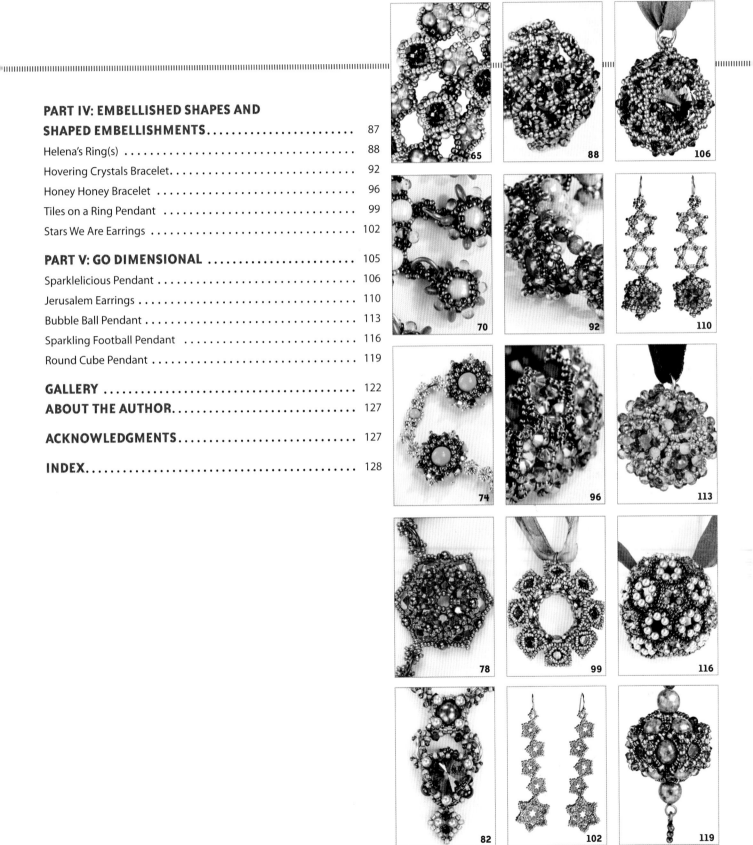

INTRODUCTION

The term "beadwork evolution" may seem a bit strange to use in the context of jewelry making, because beads are not living organisms. So why do I use this terminology? Well, the beads do not evolve, but the ways in which we use them can be quite evolutionary. Like mother nature, we are arranging a multitude of shapes and presenting a vast array styles. And again like mother nature, we are always finding out which changes work, and which ones don't.

Many new designs that we admire often look very much alike at first glance. But take a closer, second look, and you will notice subtle differences. Take the time to examine the variety found in construction, technique, color, and design. It becomes clear that each artist has her or his own beadworking style. New ideas abound, and we all influence each other and benefit from the experiences of our fellow beaders. Cooperation among artists and within the industry is continually bringing us creative shapes, variable techniques, and better quality beads and supplies. The entire beading world is in motion.

In this book I want to show the world of little changes—those clever, small variations that can make things easier, nicer, neater, or just different from the usual path.

Some time ago I had a student in a workshop who was struggling with right angle weave stitch and made a mistake on the project she was making. After looking at what she had done, I started thinking and realized that though her effort really didn't work for that particular project, her seeming error would make a great base for another technique, as you will see in Marrakech Earrings on page 48.

In other words, a mistake is not always a mistake; it can be the beginning of an entire new world! So let us continue on the successful evolutionary path of trial and error, finding which "mistakes" work, and which ones don't, in the unlimited world of beads.

BEADS, TOOLS, AND TECHNIQUES

"So many beads, so little time!"

The phrase above is well-known to beaders. But we could modify it slightly and also say, "So many bead *shapes*, so little time!" The beading world has profited in recent years as an abundance of beads and supplies have become available from all over the world. But this abundance can sometimes lead to confusion, particularly about the definition of a bead. For instance, when I talk about round beads, other people might refer to them as pearls or druk beads. Many beaders use *delica* for a cylinder bead. And while a rocaille is a silver-lined bead for some, for me it is a seed bead. So I offer the following quick overview.

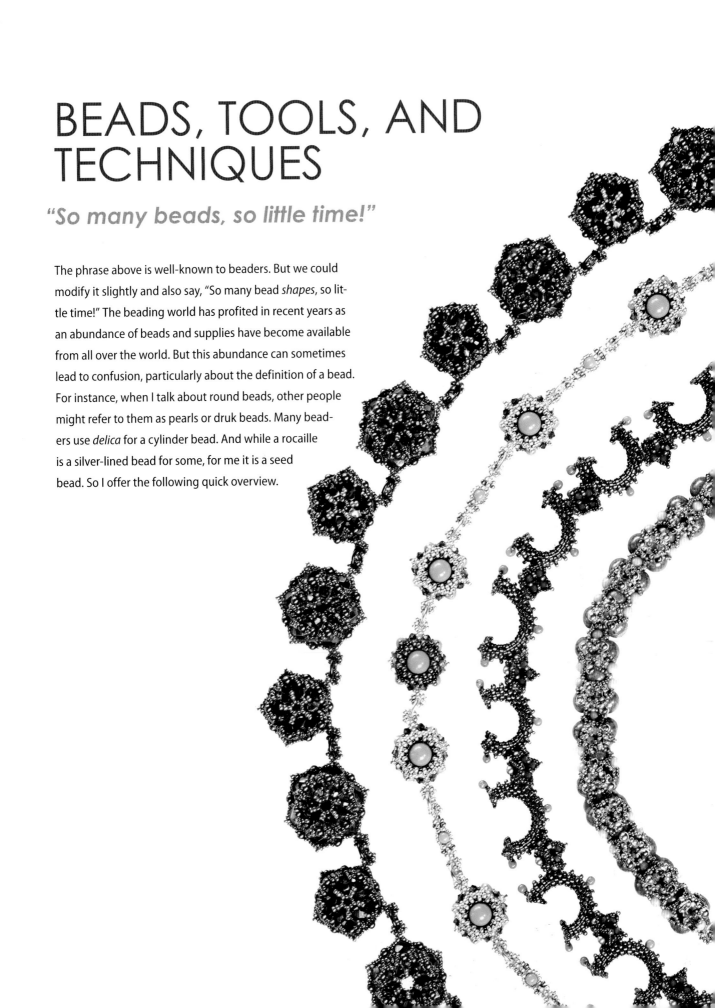

Seed Beads

Seed beads are small beads and they come from several different countries. The techniques I use in this book require seed beads of good quality, especially when it comes to uniformity of size.

Round seed beads, which are called rocaille beads in Europe, are available in sizes from 15° to 6° or larger. These will be referred to simply as seed beads throughout the book. Higher numbers designate smaller beads, thus 6° is bigger than 15°.

You will also find seed beads that are cylinder shaped. These are known as delica beads from Miyuki and treasure or aiko beads from Toho. These I will call cylinder beads throughout the book, due to their shape.

I recommend Japanese seed beads from Miyuki and Toho, but even they have their disadvantages as well as their advantages. Miyuki beads, especially the small sizes, are useful for tiny embellishments. Toho size 15° seed beads have a slightly more cylindrical shape than Miyuki seed beads, as well as a bigger hole, which makes them more suitable for bead crochet or flat peyote stitch. It is my experience, based on the many workshops I've attended, that silver-lined beads are often bigger and more cylindrical than other seed beads, which can lead to problems when you are following general instructions.

Round Beads

This sounds overly simple, but a round bead is simply any bead with a round shape, whether it has a pearl coating or is a glass bead with an AB coating. A lot of people call these druk beads, but this is a word for which I have never found a true translation. My theory is the word comes from the German *druck*, which means "pressure." So it could be a pressed bead. However, I prefer to include the shape in the name, so a round bead is a round bead, no matter which material is used (metal, crystal, pearl coating). You can find round beads in many sizes, from 2 mm and up.

Crystals

There are two different shapes of crystal beads. One, the bicone, is named for its shape: two cone-shaped structures joined on their bases. Although bicone beads can be found in smaller or larger sizes, the greatest selection for different colors are from 3 to 6 mm. The other, more faceted type of crystal is rounder in shape.

You can purchase crystals from a number of different sources, and some are much more inexpensive than others. But it doesn't always pay to save money on them. Quality crystals have additional polish on the rim of the bead hole, and your thread will be thankful for that. Crystals can be a sparkly replacement for a round bead. But be careful, every rose has its thorn—these beads, especially the cheaper brands, can cut your thread.

Rivolis and Chatons

Crystals have come to play a fundamental role in my bead-work. It always causes a big laugh in my workshops when I tell students that I was a pure seed-beader at the beginning of my beading career, with no interest in crystals at all. I found them way too "blingy."

Well, let me just say that I have since changed my mind. But there are so many different shapes of these fancy stones that I decided to focus on using rivolis and chatons.

A rivoli is a round crystal stone with a faceted front and back; both sides of the stone are equal. They come in multiple colors from 8 mm (sometimes called SS39, which stands for stone size) up to 18 mm in 2-mm increments. A chaton, on the other hand, has a partly faceted front with a flat center and comes to a tip on the back. It looks a bit like a classic diamond cut. You find the best selection of different colors for chatons in size 8 mm (SS39).

These stones can have foil on the back, which enhances the shimmer on the front. Unfoiled rivolis or chatons are paler, but can create interesting effects, especially for earrings, where you can see the light shine through.

Fire-Polished Beads

These beads have an oval shape and a number of facets. One could say they are somewhere between the round bead and the bicone. Fire-polished beads come in a multitude of colors, coatings, and finishes. They are perfect for right angle weave and as a base for a geometrical structure. It is sometimes a pity to cover them with other beads because their colors can be so beautiful. Usually fire-polished beads are 3, 4, or 6 mm. There are larger sizes, but they are more often used for stringing techniques.

Special Shapes

There has been a multitude of new bead shapes coming on the market lately, especially from Czech manufacturers, and it is always interesting to see how these shapes influence the creativity of beaders all over the world. Just think of the huge boom with spike beads or double-hole beads (also known as superduo or twin beads). One thing I love about Czech beads is the many different coatings they offer, and that makes the whole series so interesting.

Note: Unfortunately, some of these names, like superduo, are not copyright-protected, so that beads of slightly different shapes or sizes are sold under the same name. That can lead to a lot of confusion, especially when people are following instructions that require an accurate size.

One Japanese bead that should be mentioned is the drop bead, also called a fringe bead. These can be used for embellishments and also very nicely fill in corners in your beadwork.

In 2012, I was honored that my idea for a new style of bead was brought to market by a Czech manufacturer—the rizo bead, which is a long drop bead in the shape of a rice grain. It has become a nice addition to my bead stock (see Beaded Charms Bracelet, page 70; and Tips and Tops Bracelet, page 45.

Threads

Discussions about thread preference can become passionate, with some folks quite strong in their opinions on the type that is best. But in reality there is only one rule to follow: Whatever works for you is fine! When I started beading, I preferred a multifilament nylon thread (like OneG or KO thread). But since then, my standard has become FireLine, a braided thread with a coating on the surface.

Spools of FireLine can be purchased in different thicknesses and colors. The number of pounds (or kilos) indicates the thread's resistance before it will break, and crystal FireLine is less resistant than similarly sized smoke-colored FireLine, which means that 6 lb. crystal is thicker than 6 lb. smoke.

Try weaving your FireLine at least four times through a size 15° seed bead before you start making a project. If you can do so, then your FireLine is fine for making these pieces.

Needles

The needles on my work desk lead a hard life because I tend to bend them time and again, so it is really important to use ones of good quality. I have wondered why I seem to bend so many until I found out that there are different ways people hold their needles. There are the "two finger people," who hold the needle between their thumb and index finger. These folks rarely have problems with bent needles. And then there are the "three finger people," using their middle finger in addition to the thumb and index. I have to live with the fact that I am a "three finger person," and so I have to buy high-quality, relatively expensive needles, like the ones from Tulip.

Scissors

My father always used to say, "Don't save money on tools." But when you are working with FireLine, your scissors can be an exception. This thread makes every blade dull after a short time. So use either a thread burner or cheap scissors that will not hurt your wallet too much when you have to replace them. If you use nylon thread, you can of course work more precisely with a good pair of scissors.

Pliers

Here my father's rule fully applies. You cannot make a nice loop on an eye pin, or open a jump ring, when the tips of your pliers have notches from previous work. A complete set of pliers for ten dollars will not serve you well—better to spend more on quality. Also, I do not recommend that you buy pliers online. It is best to hold them and try them out to feel how they fit in your hand. Sometimes it is good to get these pliers from an electronics store.

Beaders' Little Helpers

Whenever you visit a beading retreat in Germany, where I live, you might think gummy bears are the most important extra for beaders (and I totally agree there). They are good for the nerves and they don't leave your fingers sticky, like some other candies. But sweet treats aside, there are many other little accessories that can make your beading life more comfortable. Most are not "must-haves"; rather, they are what I call "nice to haves."

I like little metal triangles to scoop my beads. There is a long side to scoop large quantities of beads, but also a tip that is small enough to sort out single beads.

Thread burners are a nice addition, especially when you want to save your scissors when using FireLine.

Beading mats and beading boards are a personal decision, but again, whatever works best for you is the way to go. A lot of beaders use simple beading mats, foam rubber mats, or plain old towels. I prefer beading boards, especially when you can stack them. Some time ago I discovered the "Bead On It Boards." Besides the fact that they are very sturdy and you can stick your needles in the rim, they simply look great and I love working on them.

Clasps

Clasps are always an individual decision. Some people prefer pure beadwork and bead their own clasps. Others sew them onto their beadwork. I prefer a technique that allows me to easily remove and exchange the clasp. Metal clasps that are not sterling silver or gold may tarnish quickly, making it necessary to replace them. The entire piece can be harmed if you need to replace clasps that have been sewn to the beadwork. Clasps are a classic "hunting and collecting" piece. If you see one you like, get it!

Before the Stitching Starts

Sometimes thread paths in drawings can illustrate an overload of information and become confusing. Because of this, I gave up drawing double thread passes for the illustrations in this book. So if you find a double thread path in the text and not in the drawing, it is to give a better overview. Double thread passes are very useful when you create netting parts. By stepping up in the next row, your tension can easily get lost. By reinforcing the beads another time, you can achieve much better tension.

Peyote Stitch

Even Count Peyote

Even count peyote is a fundamental stitch for understanding odd count peyote, which is used a number of times in this book. Imagine facing a horizontal brick wall turned 90° so it is vertical. That is similar to the pattern of this stitch.

String an even number of beads (figure 1). Because you will be adding a new bead in every second position, this first row will count as rows 1 and 2.

figure 1

Turning back as illustrated in figure 2, add one bead, skip the first bead of the previous row, and weave through the next one. Repeat this until you reach the other end of the row. The following rows are made in the same way. Note that after the third row, every other bead will be higher than its adjacent bead—these are the ones you will continue to weave through.

figure 2

The following rows are made in the same way. After the third row, you can see beads standing up; these are the beads where you weave through (figure 3).

figure 3

Odd Count Peyote

Odd count peyote is a little more involved that even count, but it is nevertheless a stitch that is rewarding.

String an odd number of beads, which will be rows 1 and 2. Turning back, add one bead, skip the first bead of the previous row, and weave through the next one. Repeat until there are only two beads left at the end. You cannot simply add a bead in the last position, because there is no bead following where you can secure it. Instead, weave through the last two beads of the previous row (figure 4).

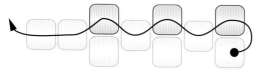

figure 4

String one bead, skip the first bead of the previous row, then weave through the next two beads of the previous row (not the bead you added before the last one; see figure 5).

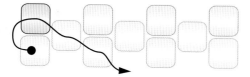

figure 5

Once the last bead of the row is added, you only need to get to the starting point for the next row. Therefore, enter the bead on top of the one you are exiting from, heading to the end of the row, and weave, like in step 1, through the last three beads (the one you added in step 1 and the last two beads of the base row [rows 1 and 2]).

Now you can enter the first bead and are in the starting position for the next row. On the other end, you will end the row as shown in even count peyote. On this end of the row, you will always end the row as shown (figure 6).

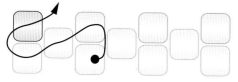

figure 6

Zipping in Peyote Technique

Zipping allows you to roll a flat strip into a secure tube. Make a flat strip using peyote stitch and take care to have an even number of rows. Then roll the strip so that the two ends come together. As shown in figure 7, the ends are like two halves of a zipper, with "teeth" that fit into matching slots. Exiting from the end of the last row, enter the first bead of the other end of your strip. Then enter the last bead added in the previous row (that bead is sticking up on the end of the strip where you started). Weave, alternating between the beads on both ends that protrude, until you reach the other end of the row. To attach the last bead, once more enter the first bead at the other end of the strip (your starting row).

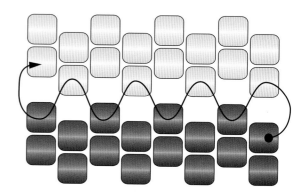

figure 7

Circular Peyote

This sophisticated stitch opens up all types of possibilities for shaped beadwork.

String an even number of beads (here 16) and make a circle by weaving again through the first beads strung. Though some beaders tie knots to secure this first loop, I do not. In my eyes, it is difficult to calculate the perfect length of the thread. When you start adding the next row, you need to push every second bead halfway down (as is usual for peyote stitch). That means your thread will follow a zigzag line. If you tie the knot too tightly, the beads of the first ring will remain in one level, and the following rows will not look very neat. If you tie it too loosely, there will be gaps. Leave about 8 inches (20 cm) of a tail, allowing you to pull it or loosen it after finishing the first rows (figure 8).

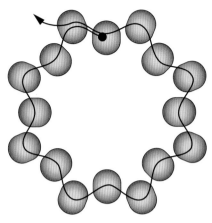

figure 8

String one bead, skip one bead in the base row, and weave through the next one. Repeat this up to the end of the circuit. Here you weave through the first bead strung in this step. This is called the step up. You have to do this to get to the starting point of the next row (figure 9).

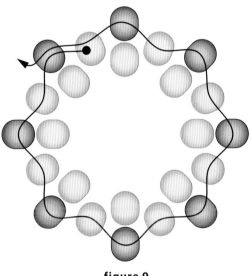

figure 9

As you can see, this starting point is going like a spiral around the tube. Each time you step up, you are going one bead further around.

Double Drop Peyote

There is a version of peyote stitch that is faster to do. Instead of stringing one bead in each position, you can string two or three beads at once. These multiples will count as one bead. Just take care to always add the same number of beads in the same vertical position.

Peyote Increases and Decreases

To make an increase in the number of beads, you can add a pair of beads in one or more of the gaps (every second gap in figure 10).

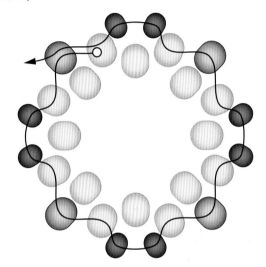

figure 10

In the next row, add one bead in each gap and also one bead in between the pairs of beads added in the previous row (figure 11).

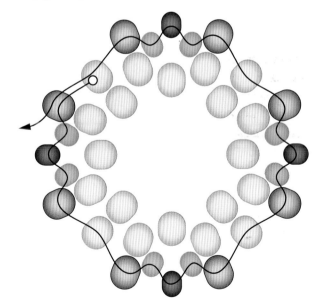

figure 11

In the next row, add one bead in each gap. As you can see, we have an increase from eight to 12 gaps by working four increases (figure 12).

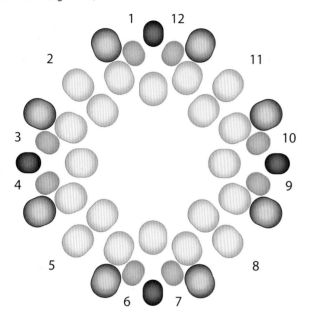

figure 12

To work a decrease, shown in a straight row in figure 13, weave through two adjacent beads sticking up in the first decrease row (figure 14). In the next row, add one bead on top of this pair joined in the previous row (figure 15).

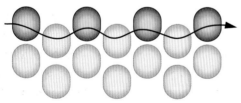

figure 13

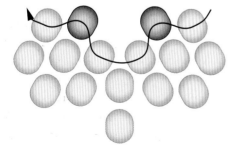

figure 14

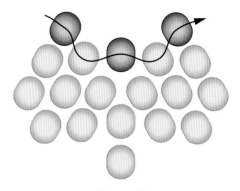

figure 15

Right Angle Weave

I've known people who seem to fear right angle weave, and I've heard it said that this stitch is the most difficult of all. Well, beads don't bite, so give it a try!

Right angle weave describes the thread path. In classic right angle weave, you never weave straight from one bead to the next. Instead, you make a kind of square, referred to as a unit, in each step. In these units, the beads are the sides of the square and the thread path makes the corner. This is sometimes difficult to notice because our eyes tend see the bead as the corner. It is easier to visually identify the square structure when using oval beads (such as fire-polished beads).

Start the first unit by stringing four beads, then make a unit of these beads by weaving again through the first one. Exiting from one bead of that unit, string three more beads, weave again through the bead where you exited, and then forward to the second bead just added. From here, continue adding three beads until the strip reaches the required length. Notice that the thread path alternates between clockwise and counter-clockwise directions (figure 16).

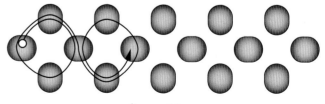

figure 16

To add a second row, exit from the first bead on the edge of the strip and string three new beads. Then weave again through the bead where you exited. Weave forward and exit from the next bead on the edge, string two new beads, and weave through the bead of the previous unit and the bead where you exited. Also work clockwise and counterclockwise here, adding two new beads in each step after the first one (figure 17).

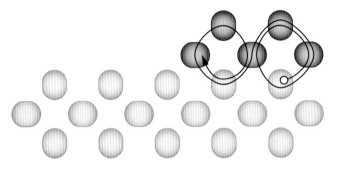

figure 17

A Faster and Easier Version of Right Angle Weave

Oh yes, it exists: a version of right angle weave that avoids the clockwise/counterclockwise pattern. I love to embellish right angle weave bases where thread is typically visible. Usually I make these embellishments after the base has been beaded, when embellishing means to add small beads in each crossing point between the beads of the lattice. For the faster version, add these beads right away.

Make a first unit as usual, but then string one smaller bead (here a 15° in a base made with 11° seed beads). After that, string three more 11°s. Then weave through the bead adjacent to the one where you exited, creating the next unit. Weave one 11° bead further (skipping the 15°) and string one more 15° followed by three 11°s. Continue making unit after unit in a similar manner. As you can see, you are beading counterclockwise in every unit (figure 18).

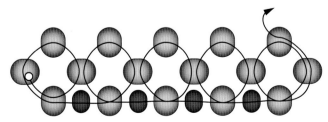

figure 18

In the next row, start the first unit by adding three 11° beads, then weave forward to the second bead on the edge by adding one 15° in between the first two beads on the edge.

Start the second unit in the second row by stringing two 11°s, then weave through the 11° of the previous unit and the 11° where you exited. Weave forward into the next bead on the edge by adding one more 15°. Note that now the thread path is always in the clockwise direction (figure 19).

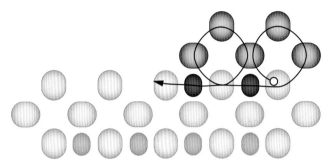

figure 19

Last But Not Least, What about the Thread?

One of the most frequent questions asked in my workshops is about how long the thread should be. My answer is always, "It should be whatever length is most comfortable for you to work with!"

Sure, you could use a 5-yard (4.6 m) piece of thread if you love to untie knots and if drama is your idea of fun as the thread gets thinner and thinner with each additional pass through a bead and finally breaks in your finished piece. Or you can always use a very short thread with a tiny tail that can only be grabbed with your pliers if you love low tension and are a maniac for adding new thread!

Seriously, though, I have a simple plan when it comes to thread—I always take one wingspan: the length from fingertip to fingertip with my arms outstretched. The tail should be at least 5 inches (12.7 cm) so you can hold it in your hand and wrap it around your fingers to retain the counter tension to your working thread. When your thread starts looking frizzed, work it off and attach a new one. Your finished piece will only be as good as the thread you are using. After spending lots of money for high-quality beads, it makes no sense to save pennies on the thread.

Working the Thread

I do not make knots in my beadwork because they are not necessary. Besides, whenever I do make a knot, you can bet it will end up in the one bead where I have to make multiple thread passes.

I understand that some beaders prefer making a knot when starting a row of circular peyote. But if the knot is tied too close, you will not be able to add the beads of the next row. Or, if the knot is too loose, the beadwork becomes wobbly. You cannot correct a knot later on. Once it is there, it can only be removed with scissors, and then you will have to start over. Knots can harm your thread and break in place. Yet despite these arguments against making knots, I also have to say, as I've done before, "Whatever works for you is fine!"

To work off the thread when weaving through the beadwork, change direction several times and pull the last beads added when you have done enough passes to see whether your thread is secure. Cut off the thread if the beads are clearly secure (figure 20).

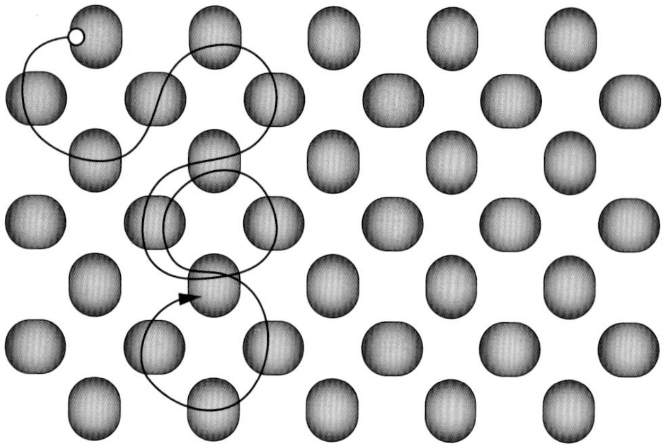

Add new thread the same way. Weave through the beadwork until the thread is secure, then continue weaving forward to the point where you want to continue.

And this is enough talk about beading—let's get started making jewelry.

Happy beading!

figure 20

I: Peyote Can Be Different

Peyote is more versatile than many beaders realize. While rather stiff in one direction, it is flexible in the other, which makes it perfect to create dimensional pieces.

SO EARRESISTIBLE EARRINGS

Bezeled beads or crystals and can be connected to other bezeled parts. And for this pair, the seed beads are the "glue" that holds the earrings together.

Refer to figure 1 for the first three steps, but note that the drawing shows only a part of the bezel. Also, you may want to refer to the basic information for circular peyote on page 14. The beads of the starting row are outlined in red.

1 Make a bezel for a rivoli. String 30 cylinder beads and make a ring by weaving again through the first bead. Stitch forward through at least half the ring to secure the thread. Continue weaving in circular peyote and add a third row, also using cylinder beads. At the end of the ring, step up and exit from the first bead added in this row. Add two rows using 15° bronze seed beads and always remember to step up after the last bead of the row.

2 Now, working on the back of the bezel, stitch back to the beads of the first row, then continue weaving the second half of the bezel. Lay the rivoli into this cup (front-side up) and weave another two rows using 15° seed beads.

3 To create the frame in front of the rivoli, continue weaving in circular peyote, adding one row with cylinder beads, two rows using 11° blue seed beads, and one row with a pair of 15° seed beads in each gap. Then weave along the beads, heading to the starting row. Exit from a cylinder bead at the "equator" of the bezel. This is the middle row made from cylinder beads only.

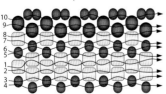

figure 1

4 String one 11° seed bead and weave through the following cylinder bead in this row. Repeat another 14 times to complete around the ring (figure 2). Secure the thread and cut it off.

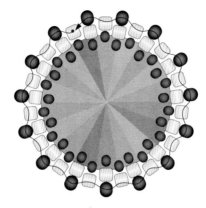

figure 2

5 To make a bezel for the first pearl (or any other round bead), string one 15° seed bead and one cylinder bead. Repeat this sequence nine times: that makes a total of 20 strung beads. Make a ring by weaving again through the first bead, then weave along the whole ring to secure the thread. Exit from a cylinder bead. String the round bead and hold it in this ring of seed beads.

To secure the round bead/pearl within the ring, exit above the ring on the opposite side and then through the pearl again from underneath. This wraps the thread once around the thread of the beaded ring, slipping into a gap between the beads. On the other side of the round bead, weave again through the cylinder bead where you started (figure 3).

figure 3

SUPPLIES

2 rivolis, 12 mm, rose peach

6 round beads, 6 mm, cream white

3 g rizo (long drop beads), 2.5 x 5.5 mm, jade dark travertine

2 g cylinder beads, 11°, light gold color

3 g seed beads, 15°, light bronze color

2 g seed beads, 11°, metallic blue

1 pair ear wires, gold color

FireLine, 6 or 8 lb

Beading needle, size 12

Fine scissors

DIMENSIONS

2¾ x 1⅜ inches (7 x 3.5 cm)

6 Exit from a cylinder bead and add one row of 15° beads using circular peyote stitch. Step up, then add another row of 15°s. Stitch back to the base row and add one more row of 15° seed beads on the back of the bezel. Stitch forward and exit from a cylinder bead on the "equator" (figure 4).

figure 4

Repeat steps 5 and 6 two more times to make bezels for your pearls or round stones.

7 Attach a bezeled round bead to the rivoli's bezel at two positions. Exit from a cylinder bead in the round's bezel and weave through an 11° seed bead on the outer row of the rivoli's bezel, then through the next cylinder bead in the round's bezel. Continue to weave through the next 11° seed bead in the rivoli's bezel and the following cylinder bead from the round/pearl unit.

figure 5

8 Continue weaving from the back. Following the black path in figure 6, exit from the first 11° seed bead where the round bezel is attached to the rivoli bezel. String two 15° seed beads and weave

through the second 11° seed bead used to attach the pearl. String two 15°s and weave through the following 11° seed bead. Add a long drop bead in each of the three gaps between 11° seed beads that follow, then one 15°, one 11° seed bead, and another 15° in the next gap. Continuing, add a long drop bead in each of the following three gaps, then two 15°

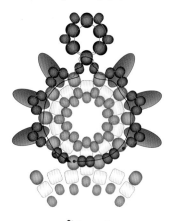

figure 6

seed beads in the last gap. Weave a second time through the beads of this row.

9 Weave forward and exit in front of the first long drop bead. Referring to the red path in figure 6, string three 15° beads, skip the drop, and weave through the following 11° seed bead. Push the three beads to form a little picot. Also push the long drop into the proper position, then pull the thread. Repeat two more times, then exit from the 11° seed bead added in the last step, opposite the position where the rivoli is attached. Add a loop here by stringing five 11° seed beads and running your needle into the bead through which you exited, then weaving a second time through the beads of the loop. Finally, add a 15° seed bead in each of the four gaps of the loop, then add three 15° seed beads behind each of the long drops, like you did on the first half of the ring.

Back

10 Referring to figure 7, count the two 11° seed beads where the first round bezel is attached to the rivoli bezel as positions one and two. Going counterclockwise to seed bead positions seven and eight, attach a second bezeled round/pearl to the rivoli's bezel as explained in step 7.

Likewise, attach a third bezeled round element at positions 10 and 11. You will end up with four blue 11°s with no attachments added to them on the left half of the bezeled rivoli, as well as four on the right half, and a single blue 11° hanging at the bottom.

11 The embellishments for the two lower elements are related to the round one at the top of the earring, but with the long drop beads placed slightly differently. Figure 7 shows the earring from the back. For the lower right element, fill the gap between the attaching beads with two 15° beads, and do the same for the next two consecutive gaps (moving counterclockwise). Place one long drop bead in each of the six following gaps, and then fill the last gap with two more 15°s. Weave a second time through the beads of the row, and finish by adding three 15° beads behind every long drop bead. Repeat in a manner that corresponds to figure 7 for the lower left element.

12 Repeat the steps to make a second earring.

Finish

Mount the ear wire with jump rings to the loops.

figure 7

HAPPY NEW YEAR NECKLACE

A project for patient beaders, this necklace is a real statement piece. Increases and decreases transform the single peyote tube into a flexible piece that is embellished with multiple crystals.

To help deal with the heft and preserve the durability of the beadwork, I strung the entire piece on a silk cord. *The easiest technique to accomplish this is to bead the entire piece around the silk cord.* If the cord has to be replaced for any reason, sew the new cord to the old one before you pull it through!

The component on each end of the necklace is bigger than any of the others. In between the two end components is a series of four differently embellished components that repeat in sequence seven times. The sequence of the colors in the base and in the embellishments are not related—they are independent.

Base

Start with the base before working along the entire necklace to add the embellishments.

All size 15° seed beads in the base are golden.

Slow Increase

In figure 1 and the following illustrations, the red dots mark the first beads in each concentric ring or circle. For the sake of consistency, each of these rings as they build on each other will be referred to as a "round." Unless otherwise indicated, the drawings show the rounds building from the inside to the outside.

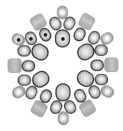

figure 1

Round 1: String six 11° seed beads (figure 1, red outlines) and make a ring, weaving two times through the beads to secure the thread.

Round 2: Add one 15° seed bead (figure 1, blue outlines) in each of the gaps from round 1. Step up and exit from the first 15° added in this round.

Round 3: String two 15° seed beads (figure 1, pink outlines) and weave through the next 15° of the second round. Repeat five times. At the end, step up and exit from the first 15° in this round.

Round 4: Add one 15° seed bead (figure 1, green outlines) and weave through the next 15° from round 3. String one green cylinder bead and weave through the first 15° seed bead of the next pair from round 3. Repeat five times to complete the round. At the end, exit from the first 15° seed bead added in this round.

Round 5: Add one green cylinder bead in each gap between cylinders and 15° seed beads from round 4 (figure 2, red outlines—due to the increases of the previous rows, there are 12 beads in this round). Exit from the first cylinder bead added in this round.

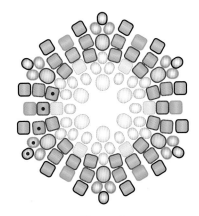

figure 2

SUPPLIES

144 bicones, 3 mm, jet, 2AB

126 round beads, 3 mm, beige

13 g seed beads, 11°, golden

15 g seed beads, 15°, golden

4 g seed beads, 15°, iris golden

33 g cylinder beads, 11°, golden

11 g cylinder beads, 11°, metallic mint green

2 ornamental metal beads, 12 mm, brass

2 ornamental metal beads, 5 mm, brass

40 inches (102 cm) silk (or fabric) cord, dark brown

FireLine, 6 lb

Beading needle, size 12

Scissors

DIMENSIONS

17½ inches (44.5 cm), not including the cord

Round 6: Add one green cylinder bead (figure 2, blue outlines) in the first gap from the previous round and one 11° seed bead in the next. Repeat five times to complete the round and exit from the first cylinder bead added.

Round 7: String one green cylinder bead (figure 2, pink outlines) and weave through the following 11° seed bead. Repeat five times to complete the round and exit from the first cylinder bead added.

Round 8: Add a pair of 15° seed beads in the first gap (figure 2, green outlines) and a green cylinder bead in the next gap. Repeat five times and exit from the first 15° added in this round.

Round 9: String one 15° seed bead (figure 2, black outlines) and weave through the following 15° seed bead from the previous round. Add a green cylinder bead in each of the next two gaps. Repeat five times to complete the round. Exit from the first cylinder bead added.

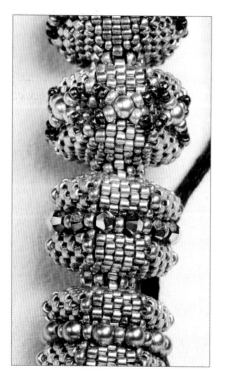

Round 10: Add one green cylinder bead in each gap (figure 3, red outlines) to total 18 cylinders in this round, and exit from the first one just added.

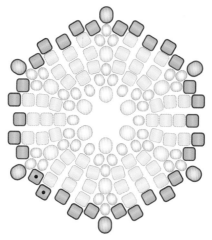

figure 3

Round 11: Add two green cylinders and one 11° seed bead in the gaps (figure 3, blue outlines). Repeat five times to complete the round and exit from the first cylinder bead added in this round.

Short Decrease

Round 12: Add one golden cylinder bead in each gap (figure 4, red outlines) all around and exit from that first bead.

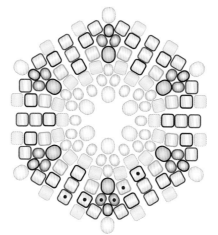

figure 4

This figure shows the rounds built from the outside to the inside.

Round 13: To work the first decrease, continue using golden cylinder beads. Add one of them in the first gap, one 15° seed bead in the second gap, and another golden cylinder in the third gap (figure 4, blue outlines). Repeat five times to complete the round and exit from the first cylinder bead added in this round.

Round 14: Add a 15° seed bead in each of the first two gaps (figure 4, pink outlines) before and after the 15° seed bead added in the previous round. Follow by adding one golden cylinder bead in the next gap. Repeat five times to complete the round. Exit from the second seed bead added in this round.

Round 15: Add a golden cylinder bead in each of the following two gaps (figure 4, green outlines), then weave through both 15° seed beads of the previous round. Repeat another five times and exit from the first cylinder bead added in this round.

Round 16: Following the beads outlined in black in figure 4, add one golden cylinder in the first gap and one 11° seed bead in the next one, above the pair of 15° seed beads added in the previous round. Exit from the first cylinder bead added.

Short Increase

Round 17: Add one golden cylinder bead in each gap (figure 5, red outlines) going around and exit from the first cylinder bead added in this round.

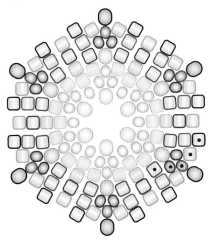

figure 5

This figure shows the rounds built from the inside to the outside.

Round 18: Add two 15° seed beads in the first gap (above the 11° seed bead) and a golden cylinder bead in the next gap (figure 5, blue outlines). Repeat five times and exit from the first of the pair of 15°s added in this round.

Round 19: Add one 15° seed bead between the first pair of seed beads added in the previous round, and a golden cylinder bead in each of the following two gaps (figure 5, pink outlines). Repeat five times and exit from the first bead added in this round.

Round 20: Add one golden cylinder bead in each gap—a total of 18 beads in this round (figure 5, green outlines)—and exit from the first cylinder bead added in this round.

Round 21: Add two golden cylinder beads and one 11° seed bead. Repeat five times to complete the round (figure 5, black outlines).

Long Decrease

Round 22: Add one golden cylinder bead in each gap (figure 6, red outlines) and exit from the first one added in this round.

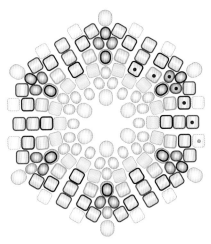

figure 6

This figure shows the rounds built from the outside to the inside.

Round 23: Add one golden cylinder bead in the first gap, one 15° seed bead in the second gap, and another golden cylinder in the third gap (figure 6, blue outlines). Repeat five times to complete the round. Exit from the first cylinder bead added in this round.

Round 24: Add a 15° seed bead in each of the first two gaps, and one golden cylinder bead in the following gap (figure 6, pink outlines). Repeat five times and exit from the second seed bead added in this round.

Round 25: Add a golden cylinder bead in each of the first two gaps and then weave through the next two 15°s (figure 6, green outlines) of the previous round. Repeat five times and exit from the first cylinder bead added in this round.

Round 26: Add one golden cylinder bead in the first gap and one golden 15° seed bead in the next one (figure 6, black outlines). Repeat five times to complete the round and exit from the first cylinder bead added in this round.

Round 27: Add one golden 15° in each gap of the round (figure 7, red outlines) and exit from the second 15° added in this round.

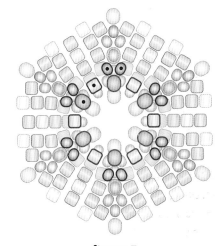

figure 7

This figure shows the rounds built from the outside to the inside.

Round 28: Add one golden cylinder bead (figure 7, blue outlines) and weave through the following two 15°s. Repeat five times and exit from the first cylinder bead added in this round.

Round 29: Add one 11° seed bead in each gap (figure 7, pink outlines). Exit from the first bead added in this round.

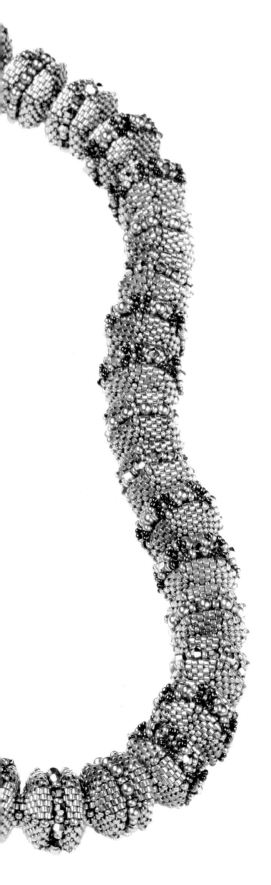

Long Increase

Round 30: Add one golden cylinder bead in each gap (figure 8, red outlines) and exit from the first cylinder added in this round.

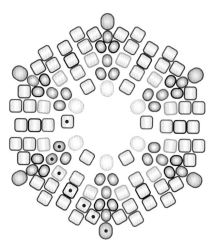

figure 8

This figure shows the rounds built from the inside to the outside.

Round 31: Add two 15° seed beads in each gap end (figure 8, inner blue outlines) and exit from the first bead added in this round.

Round 32: Add one golden 15° between the first set of 15°s paired in the previous round, followed by a golden cylinder bead (figure 8, inner pink outlines). Repeat five times and exit from the first 15° added in this round.

Round 33: Add one golden cylinder bead in each of the next 12 gaps (figure 8, green outlines) and exit from the first bead added in this round.

Round 34: Add one golden cylinder bead in the first gap and a pair of 15°s in the next one (figure 8, black outlines). Repeat five times and exit from the first cylinder bead added in this round.

Round 35: Add one golden cylinder bead, one 15° seed bead between the next pair of 15°s from the previous round, and another golden cylinder bead in the next gap (figure 8, outer red outlines). Repeat five times and exit from the first cylinder bead added in this round.

Round 36: Add one golden cylinder bead in each of the 18 gaps in this round (figure 8, outer blue outlines).

Round 37: Add one 11° seed bead above the 15° added in the previous round, and a golden cylinder in each of the next two gaps (figure 8, outer pink outlines). Repeat five times and exit from the first 11° added in this round.

Having followed all instructions for these rounds, proceed with the steps below:

1 Make a short decrease and a short increase (repeating rounds 12 through 21), only this time use golden cylinder beads in rounds 12 to 20 and green cylinder beads in round 21.

2 Make a long decrease and a long increase (rounds 22 through 37) using green cylinder beads.

3 Repeat the entire procedure thirteen times (rounds 12 through 37 and steps 1 and 2). Then work one short decrease and one short increase (rounds 12 through 21) using golden cylinder beads. Finally, work one slow decrease (rounds 1 through 11).

4 Repeat rounds 22 through 25 (long increase), but use green cylinder beads instead of golden ones. Then repeat round 26, but add 11° seed beads instead of 15°s.

At this point, make another round consisting only of golden cylinder beads. Now repeat rounds 26 through 29.

Five Embellishments

All 15° seed beads in the embellishments are iris golden. These embellishments cover the sections in the beadwork from the beginning of the short decreases to the end of the short increases. Embellishments A, B, and E are attached to the 11° seed beads added in rounds 11 and 21, at the points of the hexagon shapes.

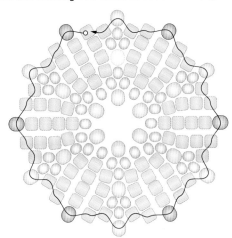

Embellishment A

5 This embellishment first requires beads added to two rounds on the base. We originally added six 11° seed beads in rounds 11 and 21. Now increase the quantity of 11° seed beads in both of those rounds to 12 by adding one bead as a stitch in the ditch between existing 11°s on all of the corners (figure 9).

figure 9

6 Referring to figure 10, exit from one 11° of round 11. String five iris golden 15°s and weave through the next 11° just added in the previous step. String five more 15°s and again weave through the next 11° from round 11. Repeat five times to complete the round and exit form the third 15° bead in the first set of five strung in this step.

figure 10

7 Again referring to figure 10, string one 15°, one bicone, and one 15°, and weave through the third 15° of the next group of five. Repeat 11 times to complete the round and exit from the second 15° bead, following the first bicone, added in this step.

8 String one 15° and weave through the following 15°, bicone, and 15° of the previous step. Repeat 11 times to complete going around. Exit from the first 15° added in this step (figure 11).

figure 11

9 String two 15°s and weave through the 11° from round 21 of the base. String two 15°s and weave through the following 15° of the previous step. String two 15°s and weave through the next 11° added to round 21 in step 12. String two 15°s and weave through the following 15° of the previous round. Repeat five times to complete the round.

Embellishment B

10 Referring to figure 12, exit from one 11° seed bead in round 37. String two 15°s, one 11°, one round bead, one 11°, and two 15°s, and weave through the following 11° of round 37. Repeat five times and exit from the first round bead added in this step.

figure 12

Again referring to figure 12, string one 11° and two 15°s, and weave through the corresponding 11° bead in round 47. String two 15°s and one 11°, and weave through the following round bead. Repeat five times to complete the round.

Embellishment C

11 Exit from an 11° of round 16, in the center between the next short decrease and increase. String one 11° and one bicone. Repeat 11 times until you have strung a total of 24 beads. Wrap the beads around the slim part between the decrease and increase, and make a ring by weaving again through the first bead strung. Weave another two or three times through the beads of the circle to secure the thread (figure 13).

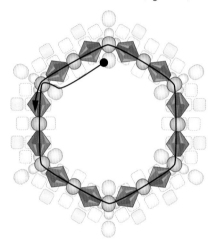

figure 13

Embellishment D

12 Make this one like embellishment C, but use round beads in place of bicones (figure 14).

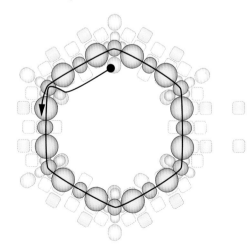

figure 14

Embellishment E

13 This one is made like embellishment B, but with bicones in place of round beads.

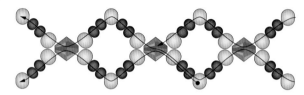

figure 15

Continue making embellishments B, C, D, and E until you reach the other end of the necklace. Finish with an A.

Finish

Secure the cord by making a knot before and after the necklace. String a 12-mm brass bead on each end of the beadwork and secure each by making a knot in the silk cord to the outside of the beads. Then string a 5-mm brass bead at each end of the silk cord and secure them with knots in the cord.

Wear the necklace by tying the silk cord using a bow knot.

CROCODILE BRACELET

Making it dimensional makes it different! Simple increases and decreases change this flat piece of peyote into a bracelet with depth and flair.

3 g drop beads, 2.8 mm, silver color

13 g cylinder beads, 11°, silver color

7 g cylinder beads, 11°, metallic rose

2 g cylinder beads, 11°, smoky pewter

0.5 g seed beads, 11°, smoky pewter

2 g seed beads, 15°, dark bronze

2 jump rings, 6 mm, 16 gauge

Magnetic clasp

FireLine, 6 or 8 lb

Beading needle, size 12

Scissors

Flat-nose pliers

DIMENSIONS

8 x 1½ inches (20.3 x 3.8 cm) not including clasp*

* Due to its cuff-like shape, this bracelet should be a little longer than standard.

Overview: Increase and Decrease

The bracelet is made in odd count peyote (see page 14). The shape is created by a combination of increases and decreases. To create an increase, add two 15° seed beads in the first row. In the back row, add one 15° seed bead in between the previous two. In the following row, add cylinder beads in each gap (figure 1).

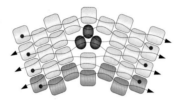

figure 1

A decrease is created by adding one 15° seed bead in the first row. In the next row, add one 15° before and one after that position. In the third row, weave through both 15° seed beads. Then, in the following row, add one cylinder bead above that position (figure 2).

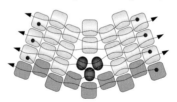

figure 2

Weave the Rows

Refer to figure 3 on the next page for all of the following instructions. The dotted lines in the figure show rows, not the thread path.

1 String 29 size 11° metallic rose-colored cylinder beads to make rows 1 and 2. Repeat to make rows 3 and 4.

2 Start the fifth row with one 11° rose cylinder bead, three 11° silver-colored cylinder beads, one 11° smoky pewter cylinder bead, two 11° silver cylinders, one 15° dark bronze seed bead, two 11° silver cylinders, one 11° pewter cylinder, three 11° silver cylinders, and one 11° rose cylinder.

For the sixth row, begin with six 11° silver cylinder beads, two 15° seed beads (positioned before and after the bronze seed bead in the previous row), and six 11° silver cylinder beads.

Moving to row 7, add one 11° rose cylinder, one 11° silver cylinder, and two 15°s. Continue with one 11° silver cylinder, one 11° pewter cylinder, and two 11° silver cylinders, then weave through both 15° bronze beads from the previous row. Add two 11° silver cylinders, one 11° pewter cylinder, one 11° silver cylinder, two 15°s, one 11° silver cylinder, and one 11° rose bead.

3 Add two 11° silver cylinder beads to start row 8, then add one 15° so it is between the two 15°s in row 7. Then add nine silver cylinder beads so that the middle one is above the pair of 15°s you wove through in the previous step. Add one more 15°, and finish the row with two 11° silver cylinder beads.

The ninth row will consist of all cylinder beads. Start by adding one 11° rose followed by four 11° silvers and one 11° pewter, then four more 11° silvers and one 11° pewter, and complete the row with four 11° silvers and one 11° rose.

In the 10th row, add seven 11° silver beads, one 15°, and seven more 11° silvers.

Start the 11th row with one 11° rose bead, four 11° silver cylinders, one 11° pewter cylinder, and another 11° silver. Continue with two 15° seed beads—one before and one after the 15° in the previous row. Complete the 11th row with

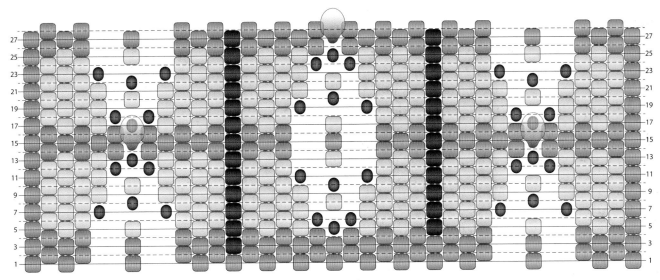

figure 3

cylinder beads as follows: one 11° silver, one 11° pewter, four 11° silver, and one 11° rose.

4 Add two 11° silver cylinder beads for the 12th row. Then add two 15° seed beads and four silver cylinder beads. Weave through the next two 15°s of the previous row, then add four 11° silver cylinder beads, two 15°s, and two more 11° silver cylinders.

Beginning row 13, add one 11° rose, two 11° silver cylinders, one 15° between the pair of 15°s in the previous row, two 11° silver cylinder beads, one 11° pewter, three more 11° silvers, one 11° pewter cylinder, two 11° silvers, one 15° between the two 15°s of the previous row, two 11° silvers, and one 11° rose bead.

5 Continuing to follow figure 3, make the 14th row by adding 16 size 11° rose cylinders.

In row 15, add three rose beads, one 2.8-mm silver drop bead, two rose beads, one 11° pewter cylinder, three 11° rose cylinders, another 11° pewter cylinder, two 11° rose beads, one more drop bead, and three 11° rose beads. The drop beads head to the front. This row is the "top of the mountain"—the beads as viewed from the front are in a convex position with the heads of the drop beads to the front.

Make the 16th row by adding 16 rose beads.

6 Start row 17 with one 11° rose bead, two 11° silver cylinders, one 15° (positioned above the first drop bead strung in row 15), two 11° silver cylinder beads, one 11° pewter cylinder, three 11° silvers, one 11° pewter cylinder, two 11° silvers, one 15° (above the second drop bead in row 15), two 11° silvers, and one 11° rose.

For row 18, add two silver 11° cylinder beads, two 15°s (one before and one after the 15° in the previous row), eight 11° silver cylinders, two 15°s (before and after the 15° in the previous row), and two 11° silver cylinder beads.

7 Start the next row with one 11° rose and two 11° silver cylinder beads and weave through both 15°s in the previous row. Continue with two 11° silvers, one 11° pewter cylinder, and one silver bead. Add a pair of 15°s in the next gap, then one silver cylinder, one pewter cylinder, and two silver cylinders, and weave through the next two 15°s in the previous row. Follow with two 11° silver cylinder beads and one 11° rose.

In the 20th row, add seven 11° silver cylinders, then one 15° between the pair of 15°s strung in the previous row. Complete the row with seven 11° silver cylinders.

Begin row 21 by adding one 11° rose bead, then four 11° silver beads, one 11° pewter, four 11° silver, one 11° pewter, four 11° silvers, and one 11° rose.

For row 22, add two 11° silver cylinders, one 15°, nine 11° silver cylinders, another 15°, and two more 11° silvers.

8 Now at the 23rd row, add one 11° rose bead, one 11° silver bead, two 15°s (one before and one after the 15° in the previous row), one 11° silver, one 11° pewter cylinder, four 11° silvers, one 11° pewter, one 11° silver, two 15°s (one before and one after the next 15° in the previous row), one 11° silver, and one 11° rose.

For row 24, add two 11° silver beads and weave through the two 15°s in the previous row. Add four 11° silver beads, two 15°s, and four 11° silvers, and then weave through the next two 15°s in the previous row. Complete the row with two silver cylinder beads.

In the 25th row, start with one 11° rose bead, three 11° silver cylinder beads, one 11° pewter cylinder, two more 11° silvers, and one 15° between the pair of 15°s in the previous row. Continue with two more 11° silver beads, another 11° pewter cylinder, three 11° silvers, and one 11° rose.

9 Still following figure 3, make row 26 by adding 14 size 11° rose beads.

For row 27, add four 11° rose, one 11° pewter cylinder, two 11° rose, and one 2.8-mm silver drop bead that will face out from the front of the bracelet. Continue with two more 11° rose cylinders, one 11° pewter cylinder, and four 11° rose beads. This row is the "valley"—the beads should form a concave shape when viewed from the front.

In the 28th row, add 14 size 11° rose beads.

10 Repeat rows 5 through 28 until you reach the desired length, except in the last repeat. To end the bracelet, work only rows 5 through 25 on the last section, then string four rows of exclusively 11° rose cylinders.

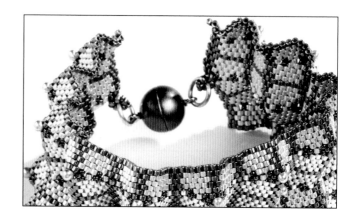

11 Start from the 15° seed bead found in the middle of the fifth row (or in the 25th row at the other end of the bracelet) and add a loop. Exit from that 15°, string five 11° smoky pewter seed beads, and pass through the 15° again to form a loop. Pass back through all these to strengthen the loop. Then add one 15° bead in each of the four gaps between the 11° seed beads. Repeat at the other end of the bracelet to make a second loop.

Finish

Mount the clasp with jump rings to the loops.

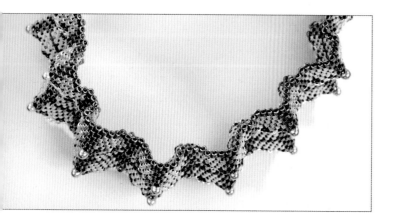

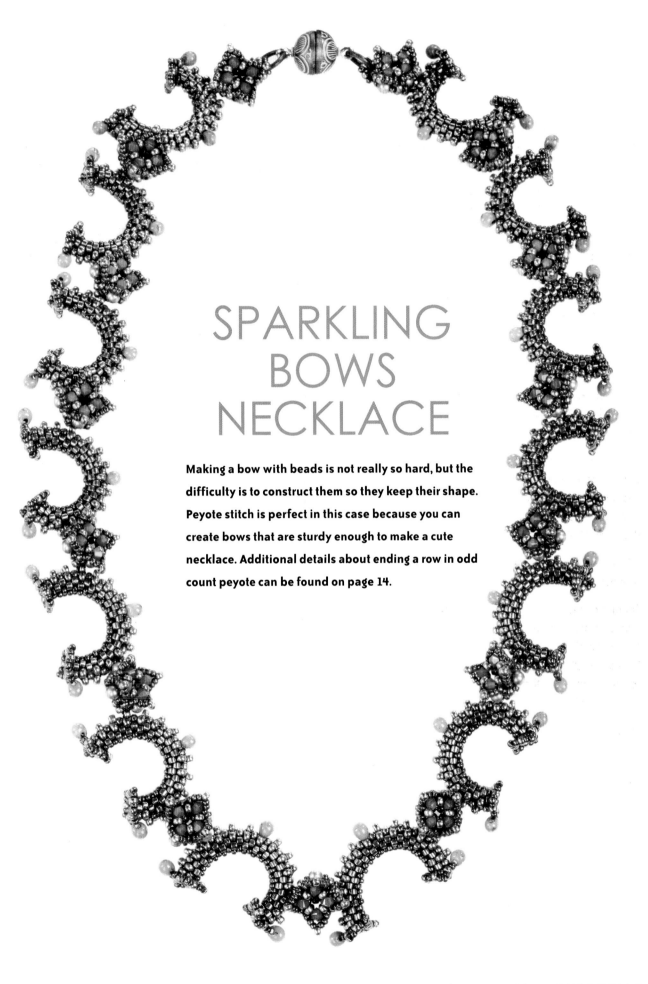

SPARKLING BOWS NECKLACE

Making a bow with beads is not really so hard, but the difficulty is to construct them so they keep their shape. Peyote stitch is perfect in this case because you can create bows that are sturdy enough to make a cute necklace. Additional details about ending a row in odd count peyote can be found on page 14.

SUPPLIES

60 bicones, 3 mm, opal green

60 round beads, 3 mm, rose

3 g drop beads, 3.4 mm, turquoise Picasso

12 g seed beads, 11°, metallic rose

8 g seed beads, 15°, light bronze

5 g cylinder beads, 11°, pewter

2 jump rings, 5 mm, 16 gauge, antique gold

1 magnetic clasp, 10 mm

Beading needle, size 12

FireLine, 0.12 mm, 6 lb, smoke

Scissors

Chain-nose pliers

DIMENSIONS

1¾ inches (47.6 cm) long, not including clasp

1 Take a wingspan of thread and start in the middle of it so that your working thread and tail are nearly the same length. String 27 size 15° seed beads (these are rows 1 and 2). For row 3, weave back in peyote stitch and again use 15° seed beads. Work the odd count peyote turn at the end of this row. Make sure the tension is not too tight in these first three rows.

Work another two rows using cylinder beads, and finally two rows with 11° seed beads (figure 1).

2 Start working with the tail. Again beginning from the first row (15° beads), work in the other direction, adding two rows with cylinder beads and one row with 11° seed beads (figure 2).

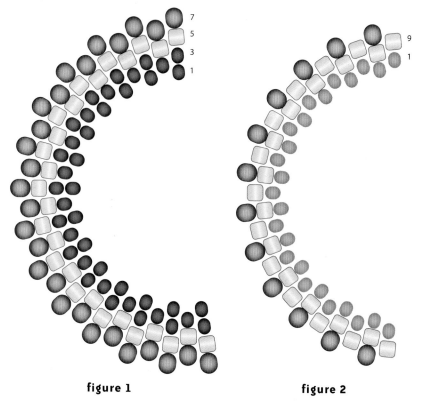

figure 1   figure 2

3 The beadwork starts to curve due to the increase of bead size. Zip together rows 10 and 7 by weaving along and alternating through the beads of these two rows (figure 3).

figure 3

4 Both threads are now ending on one end of the arch. Take the shorter end and continue. Exiting from one bead at the end, string one 15° and weave back into the same bead where you exited. Then stitch out of the end through the adjacent bead. Repeat on all five beads on the end and exit from one newly added 15° (figure 4, red outlines) in the end.

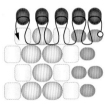

figure 4

5 Continue working in a circle. String one 11° seed bead and weave through the following 15°. Repeat four times to complete the row (figure 5, solid black path). At the end, exit from the first 11° added in this step.

In the next row, string two 15° seed beads and weave through the following 11° of the previous row. Repeat four times and exit between the first pair of 15°s added in this row (figure 5, broken black path).

figure 5

In the last row, add one 15° in the middle of each pair of 15°s from the previous row. In the one tip that is heading to the outside of the arch, use a drop bead instead of a 15° (figure 5, green outlines

and path). Weave another time through the beads of this last row and secure the thread. Then cut it off and continue with the other thread.

6 Weave through the beads, so your thread exits from an 11° in the opposite direction. String one 11° and weave through the following 11° bead of row 8 of the peyote base. Repeat five times, but add a drop bead instead of an 11° in the seventh position, then continue adding six more 11°s (figure 6).

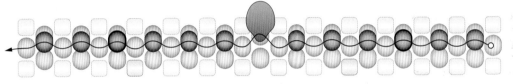

figure 6

Exiting on the other end of the arch, repeat steps 4 and 5. Do not cut off the thread.

7 Notice the two 11° beads, third from each end, outlined in black in figure 6. These beads are used to make links between the arches of the necklace. They are also outlined in black in figure 7.

After finishing a second arch, connect it to the previous one by exiting from one of the 11° beads outlined in black in one of the two arches. String three 11°s and make a right angle weave unit by weaving again through the bead where you started. Follow that by exiting from the second bead added and making another right angle weave unit using 11° beads. Connect this to the other arch by stringing an 11° and weaving through the corresponding 11° bead (third from the end) on that arch, then add one more 11° and weave again through the bead where you started (figure 7).

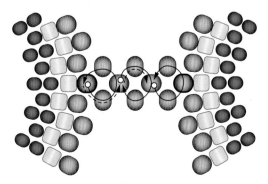

figure 7

8 Weave along the outside edge of the link make in step 7 and add four 11° beads as illustrated by the green outlines in figure 8, one before and one after the 11° bead in the middle of both sides of the link.

Weave another time through all the beads to tighten the thread and secure the link. Exit from one of newly added 11°s.

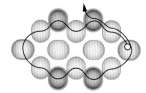

figure 8

9 Make right angle weave units on all four 11°s added in the previous step. Do this by stringing one 15°, one 11°, and another 15°, then weaving again through the 11° where you exited. Continue to stitch forward and repeat for each of the other three beads (figure 9). Exit from the 11° of one right angle weave unit added in this step.

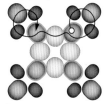

figure 9

10 String two 15° beads, one bicone, and two 15°s, and weave through the following 11° of the previous step. Repeat three times and exit from the first bicone added in this step.

String one 11° and weave through the following bicone. Repeat three times, pulling the bicones closer together. Weave a second time through the beads of this last (inner) row (figure 10).

figure 10

11 Exit from a 15° in front of a bicone. String four 15°s, skip the bicone, and weave through the following two 15°s, 11°, and two 15°s. Repeat three times to complete the row (figure 11, black path) and exit from the second 15° added in this step.

Continue by stringing one 11° and weaving through the following four 15°s. Skip the 11° of step 9 and weave through the next four 15°s (figure 11, red path). Repeat the step three times.

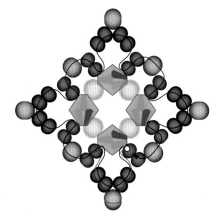

figure 11

12 Weave back to the beads of step 9 and exit from an 11°. String one 15°, one round bead, and another 15°, and weave through the following 11° bead of step 9. Repeat three times and weave again through the beads of this step (figure 12). Secure the thread and cut it off.

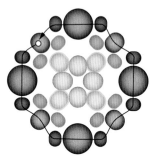

figure 12

13 Make additional arches and connect each to the previous one following steps 7 through 12 until the necklace reaches the desired length. The links at the ends of the first and last arches each end in a loop. For these, make the basic right angle weave link but do not connect to an arch. Instead, starting from the 11° at the end of this link, string five 11° beads and weave another time through the bead where you exited from. Weave again through the beads of the loop to tighten the thread, then weave a third time through the loop, this time adding a 15° bead in the second, third, fourth, and fifth gaps between the 11° beads (figure 13).

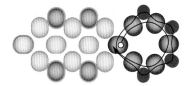

figure 13

Finish

Mount the clasp to the loops by using jump rings.

II: Right Angle Weave and Variations

It is often said that right angle weave is the most difficult stitch, but one worth mastering. Part of its value lies in the fact that it allows for the greatest number of variations among all stitches. No other allows you to mix different sizes and shapes of beads so easily.

RINGS AND
SPOTS NECKLACE

One valuable attribute of circular right angle weave is its versatility.
By using different bead sizes, you can create increases and decreases
without changing the bead count. This necklace showcases easy-to-
make rings connected with bezeled chatons.

Make the Rings

1 String four 11° seed beads and make a right angle weave unit by weaving again through the first one. Weave another time through the beads. Exiting from one of the beads, string three more 11° seed beads and weave again through the bead where you exited the first unit. Weave forward and exit from the second bead just added.

Repeat 12 times to make a strip of 14 right angle weave units. Close the strip to form a ring by exiting from the 11° bead at the end of the strip. String another 11° seed bead, weave through the 11° at the other end of the strip, and then string one more 11° seed bead and weave again through the bead where you started (figure 1).

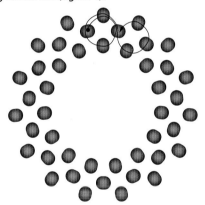

figure 1

Exit from one of the beads on the outside edge. This set of units will end up as the inside of a finished ring in this necklace.

2 Weave along the outside edge of the ring and add one cylinder bead in each gap. At the end, exit from the seed bead where you started (figure 2).

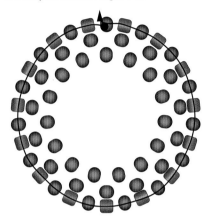

figure 2

3 String one 11° seed bead, one 8° seed bead, and another 11° seed bead, then weave again through the 11° seed bead where you exited.

Weave forward through the following cylinder bead and 11° seed bead before exiting and stringing another 11° seed bead and an 8°. Weave through the 11° seed bead of the previous unit and the 11° where you exited. Repeat until you have finished 14 units along the outside edge of the original ring. To complete the last unit, weave forward through the 11° seed bead of the previous row and also through the next 11° seed bead of the first unit made in this step. String one 8° bead to complete the last (15th) unit (figure 3).

SUPPLIES

15 chatons, 8 mm (SS39), Indian red

10 g seed beads, 8°, red metallic

17 g seed beads, 11°, red metallic

4 g seed beads, 15°, light bronze

5 g cylinder beads, 11°, metallic muscat

2 jump rings, 5.5 mm, 16 gauge

Magnetic clasp

FireLine, 0.12 mm, 6 lb

Beading needle, size 12

Scissors

Chain-nose pliers

DIMENSIONS

16¾ inches (42.5 cm) long, not including clasp

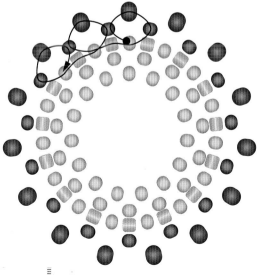

figure 3

4 Weave back to the base ring from step 1 and exit from an 11° seed bead at the other edge. Add one cylinder bead in each gap (like you did in step 2) and exit from the 11° bead where you started this step (figure 4).

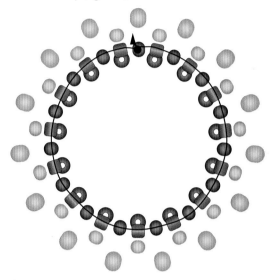

figure 4

5 Following figure 5, zip the row where you are exiting from with the row of 8° beads. Exit from a size 11°, string one 11, weave through the corresponding 8° on the outside edge of the ring. Then string one more 11° seed bead and weave again through the bead where you exited to start this step.

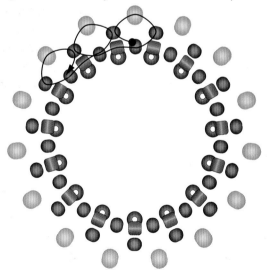

figure 5

Weave forward through the following cylinder bead and 11° seed bead. String an 11° seed bead, then weave through the size 8° on the other edge, the 11° seed bead of the previous unit, and the first 11° strung in this step. Continue zipping in this manner all the way around, but do not add new beads to the last unit. Instead, weave through the 11° seed bead of the first unit, the 8° of the other edge, and the 11° seed bead of the previous unit.

6 There are still gaps between the 8° beads along the edge of the ring you have just formed. Fill these not by weaving straight along the outline, but by weaving from one side of the ring to the other.

Exit from an 11° seed bead, heading toward the gap between two 8° beads. String three 15° seed beads, skip the gap between the two 8°s, and weave through the three 11° seed beads on the other side. Weave forward along the three 11° seed beads of the right angle weave unit and exit in front of the next gap between the following two 8° beads. As illustrated in figure 6, follow this zigzag course to weave along the entire outline and fill the gaps as shown.

The first ring of the necklace is now finished. Leave a bit of thread to make a loop later on and cut off the tail.

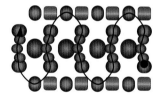

figure 6

7 Make a second ring following steps 1 through 6 and exit from an 8° bead.

8 To connect the two rings, start by stringing an 8° bead and weaving through an 8° bead of one of the rings. Following a circular path, string another 8° seed bead and weave through an 8° bead in the second ring, then weave again through the bead where you started, creating a right angle weave unit that joins the rings (figure 7). Weave at least another two times through the four beads of this unit to secure the thread.

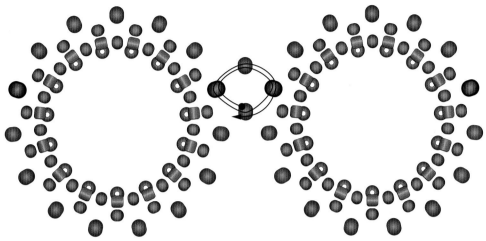

figure 7

9 Starting from the four 8° beads in the joining unit, create a chaton bezel by stringing one 15° bead, one 11° seed bead, and another 15°. Then weave through the next 8° bead. Repeat three times to complete a ring. At the end, exit from the first 11° strung in this step (figure 8).

10 String three 11° seed beads and weave again through the 11° where you exited. Weave forward along the beads in the row to the 11° seed bead in the next corner. Repeat three times to complete going around. At the end, exit from the second 11° in the group of three first added in this step (figure 9).

11 String four cylinder beads and weave through the middle bead in the following group of three 11° seed beads (figures 9 and 10, black outlines). Repeat three times to complete going around. Loosen the thread and place the chaton in the bezel, front-side up. Pull the thread and weave another time through the beads of this circle, but skip the 11° seed beads in the corners (figure 10).

12 Exit from one of the 11° seed beads in a corner and string one 15°, one 11° seed bead, one 8°, another 11° seed bead, and another 15°, then weave through the 11° seed bead in the next corner. Repeat three times to complete this round, weaving several times through these beads to secure the thread, then cut it off (figure 11).

figure 8

figure 9

figure 10

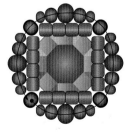

figure 11

Connect the Rings

13 The necklace is made of 16 connected rings and requires a gentle curve around the neck to keep it from flipping or twisting when worn, so it is important to attach each ring in the proper position. There should always be five 8° beads visible on the inside edge of a ring between the connecting bezeled chaton units, and eight 8° beads on the outside edge between the connecting units.

14 Attach a beaded loop to the first and last rings of the necklace. Do this by exiting from the 8° bead in those two rings where you would normally add the chaton bezel. String five 11° seed beads and weave again through the 8° bead where you exited. Weave a second time through the beads of the loop, then a third time through and add a 15° in the second, third, fourth, and fifth gaps between the 11°s (figure 12).

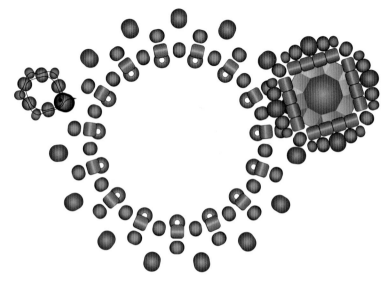

figure 12

Finish

Mount the clasp with a jump ring on each loop at the beginning and end of the necklace. If you want to create a bracelet variation of this piece, start with a basic circle of 16 units and connect the rings in a straight line with the chaton bezels.

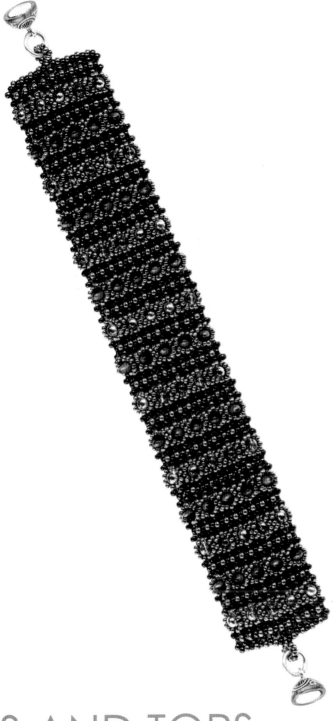

SUPPLIES

3 g drop beads 3.4 mm, crystal marea

3 g rizo (long drop beads), 2.5 x 5.5 mm, jet matte sunset

9 g seed beads, 11°, brown

4 g seed beads, 11°, bronze

3 g seed beads, 15°, bronze

2 jump rings, 5 mm, 16 gauge, gold color

Magnetic clasp

FireLine, 0.12 mm, 6 lb, smoke

Beading needle, size 12

Scissors

Chain nose-pliers

DIMENSIONS

7 inches (17.8 cm) long, not including clasp

TIPS AND TOPS BRACELET

Save time by making the base and the embellishment of right angle weave all in one step. Larger beads are part of the base, while gaps between the beads are filled in the primary stitch.

1 Make a strip by starting the first row using right angle weave, but instead of the classic stitch (unit by unit, alternating beading directions), go from one unit to the next by adding a bridge bead.

To do this, string four brown 11° seed beads and make a ring by weaving again through the first bead.

String one bronze 11° seed bead (bridge bead) and then three brown seed beads to make the second unit by weaving through the adjacent brown seed bead of the first unit, and then forward through the first brown bead of this second unit, skipping the bridge bead (figure 1).

Repeat by adding another bridge bead and three brown beads, continuing the pattern until you have 10 right angle weave units and nine bridge beads in between. Exit from the third brown bead of the last unit, heading away from the row of bridge beads.

figure 1

2 Following the direction shown in figure 2, add a second row. String three brown 11° beads and weave again through the bead where you exited in step 1.

String a bronze bridge bead and weave through the following brown 11° on the edge of the first row. String two more brown 11°s and weave through the adjacent brown bead in the previous unit. Skip the bridge bead and weave again through the bead on the edge of the first row where the thread exited from.

As illustrated in figure 2, continue by repeating from the point of adding a bronze bridge bead until you reach the end of the row.

To start the next row, exit from the second brown 11° of the last unit, again heading into the middle of the beadwork.

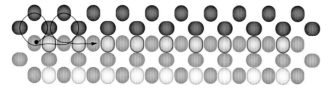

figure 2

3 For row 3, note the direction illustrated in figure 3. String a drop bead and two brown 11°s, and weave again through the 11° where you exited step 2. String one bronze 11°, again as a bridge bead, and weave through the following brown 11° of the previous row. Continue with a second unit, stringing two brown 11°s and weaving through the drop and the 11° where you exited from (skipping the bridge bead).

As shown in figure 3, continue as follows, repeating until you reach the end of the row. Make the next unit by adding a bridge bead and stringing one drop bead and a brown 11°. Then make the following unit by adding a bridge bead and stringing two 11° brown beads.

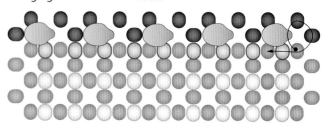

figure 3

4 Add a fourth row as described in step 2 (figure 4, solid path), exiting from the brown 11° bead that follows the last bridge bead. Weave along the beads at the end of the previous row and exit from the first bridge bead there, heading this time back to the middle of the beadwork (figure 4, broken path).

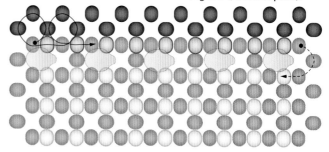

figure 4

5 Next, make rings using 15° seed beads around the drop beads. To do so, exit from the bridge bead that is next to the first drop bead, as illustrated in figure 5.

String five 15° beads, skip the drop bead, and weave through the bridge bead on the other side of the drop bead. String five more 15° beads and weave again through the bridge bead where you started. Weave forward along the beads between the second and third rows and exit from the bridge bead next to the following drop bead.

Repeat until all the drop beads are surrounded by a circle of 15°s (figure 5).

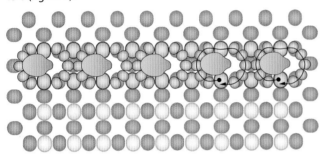

figure 5

6 Weave back to the beads of the fourth row and exit from the first brown 11° to start the following row, heading to the middle of the bracelet. Add this row as shown in step 2. Then add another row as shown in step 4, but use the rizo beads instead of the drop beads. Next, add another row like that made in step 2 and surround the rizo beads with 15° seed beads, as shown in step 5 (figure 6).

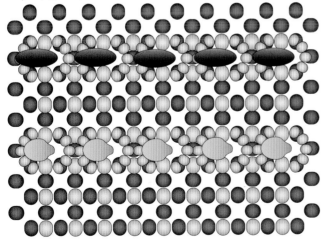

figure 6

7 Add a loop at the beginning and the end of the bracelet. Starting from the bridge bead in the middle of the row, string five bronze 11°s and weave again through the 11° from which you started. Weave a second time through the beads of the loop, and then add a 15° seed bead in the second, third, fourth, and fifth gaps of the loop. Repeat steps 2 through 6 until the bracelet reaches the desired length, and end with one row of seed beads (step 2).

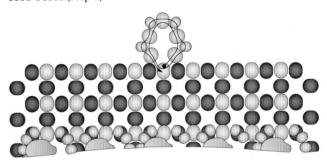

figure 7

Finish

Use jump rings to attach the clasp to the loops.

SUPPLIES

2 rivolis, 14 mm, heliotrope

8 bicones, 4 mm, purple velvet 2AB

8 round beads, 4 mm, gold-violet luster

2 g seed beads, 11°, metallic violet

2.5 g seed beads, 15°, yellow gold

2 ear wires, gold color

FireLine, 6 or 8 lb, smoke

Beading needle, size 12

Chain-nose pliers, depending on the kind of ear wires used

DIMENSIONS

1 x 1 inches (2.5 x 2.5 cm)

MARRAKECH EARRINGS

A minor mistake made by a student during a workshop led to this technique. Two little right angle weave units, starting from a simple ring of seed beads, create a perfect setting for a bicone or a round bead in this pair.

Note: Weave two times through every beaded unit in order to stabilize the construction of this pair. This extra weaving is not shown in the drawings so that the illustrations are not cluttered and easier to follow.

1 String eight 11° seed beads and make a circle by weaving again through the first bead. Weave a second time through all the beads of that circle.

2 String one 15° seed bead, one 11° seed bead, and another 15° and weave again through the bead where you exited. Weave a second time through these beads and exit from the 11° you just added (figure 1).

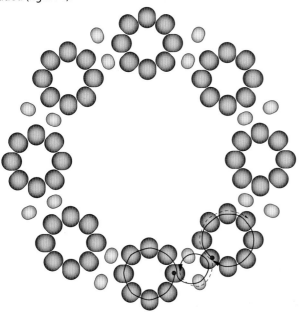

figure 1

3 String seven 11° beads and weave again through the 11° you exited in step 2. Weave a second time through these beads and exit from the fourth bead you added to start this new circle.

4 Repeat steps 2 and 3 another six times to make a strip consisting of eight small circles connected with right angle weave units. Make a base ring from this strip by connecting the last circle of 11°s to the first. To do this, continue by stringing one 15° bead and then weave through the matching bead of the first circle, and string another 15°. Weave again through the bead where you started this connection. Make sure this larger ring of smaller circles is not twisted. Again, weave a second time through the beads of the last unit. Exit from an 11° where you closed the strip of circles to form the ring.

5 Create a bezel for a round bead by stringing one 15° bead, one 11° bead, and another 15°, and weave again through the bead you exited at the end of step 4. Weave a second time through this new unit. Then, as shown in figure 2, weave along the beads of the original circle to repeat the step on the opposite side. These two right angle weave units are the mounting units. Exit from the 11° of one of these mounting units.

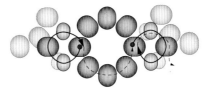

figure 2

6 String one round bead and weave through the 11° of the other mounting unit. Weave back through the round bead, then again through the bead where you started. Weave a second time through the beads of this step and exit from the 11° of one mounting unit (figure 3).

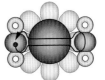

figure 3

7 String six 15°s, skipping the round bead, and weave through the following 11°. String six more 15°s and weave through the starting 11°, as illustrated in figure 4, then weave a second time through the beads of this circle.

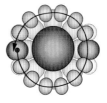

figure 4

8 Create another bezel as in step 5 on an adjacent circle of 11°s, this time for a bicone. However, do not start from the beads on the left and right positions of the small circle, but from the top and bottom, as illustrated in figure 5. As before, make a mounting unit at both positions.

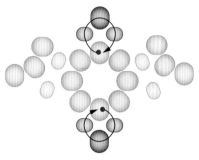

figure 5

9 String a bicone between the two mounting units as you did for the round bead in step 6 (figure 6, black path). Then string six 15° seed beads, skipping the bicone, and weave through the following 11°. Repeat on the other side of the bicone (figure 6, solid green path) and weave a second time through the beads of the circle. Exit from the third 15° added in this step (figure 6, broken green path).

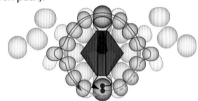

figure 6

10 String one 15° and weave through the following three 15°s, the following 11°, and the next three 15°s (figure 6, red path). Add another 15° on this side of the bicone.

11 Make another round bead bezel on the next circle, then a bicone bezel. Repeat, alternating bezels for round beads and bicones, until the basic ring formed in step 4 is covered with four round bead bezels and four bicone bezels.

12 Weave back to the base ring (faded figure 7 shows the reverse side of the ring). Exit from an 11° of one small circle, heading to the center of the base ring (figure 7, black path).

13 String two 15° beads, one 11°, and two 15°s, then weave through the corresponding 11° of the next circle. Repeat seven times, then weave forward along the beads and exit from the first 11° added in this step.

14 Referring to the red path in figure 7, string two 15°s and weave through the next 11° added in the previous round. Repeat seven more times to complete going around.

Weave another two times through the beads of the last row to secure the thread.

figure 7

15 Following the green path in figure 7, add a loop by starting from an 11° bead and stringing five 11°s heading toward the outside of the circle. Weave again through the 11° where you started, then a second time through the beads of this loop. Then weave a third time through the beads and add one 15° in the gaps between the 11°s, as illustrated.

16 Weave back to the front side and exit from the 11° of one of the bicone mounting units, heading toward the center of the ring. As shown by the black path in figure 8, string eight 15° beads and weave through the corresponding bead of the next bicone bezel. Repeat three times. Loosen the thread and place one of the rivolis face up into the vessel, then pull the thread and weave a second time through these beads to tighten. Weave once more, this time skipping the 11° beads in the four corners of the square you have formed.

figure 8

Finish

Make a second earring in the same way, then mount both earrings to the ear wires.

TRIPLE EMBRACES BRACELET

Sometimes the basic technique in a pattern isn't where you would expect. Here the primary stitch is in the big round beads. The embellishment fixes and shapes it.

1 String one 8-mm round bead followed by one 4-mm round bead. Repeat two times so that you have six alternating beads on the needle. Make a small ring by weaving again through all the beads and exit from a 4-mm round bead (figure 1).

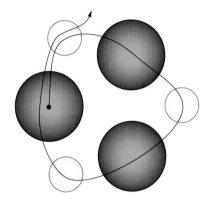

figure 1

2 String five 15° beads, one 11°, and five more 15°s, then skip the 8-mm round bead and weave through the following 4-mm round bead. Repeat two times to complete the round, making small arcs (figure 2).

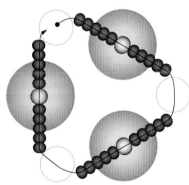

figure 2

3 Weave forward and exit from one of the 11° beads. String one 11°, one bicone, and one 11°. Weave through the 11° bead that is in the middle of the row above the next round bead. Repeat two times to complete the round (figure 3).

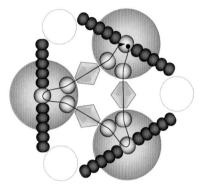

figure 3

4 Exit from a bicone and string one 15°, then weave through the following bicone. Repeat two times to complete the round (figure 4).

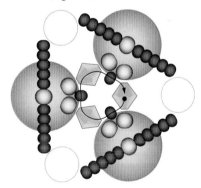

figure 4

5 Starting from a bicone, weave through the following 11° and exit. String a drop bead, skip the 11° of step 2, and weave through the following 11°, bicone, and

SUPPLIES

35 round beads, 8 mm, sea green

36 round beads, 4 mm, ivory

42 bicones, 3 mm, air blue opal 2AB

2 g drop beads, 3.4 mm, crystal silver

4 g seed beads, 11°, silver

4 g seed beads, 15°, sea green

2 jump rings, 5 mm, 16 gauge, silver

1 magnetic clasp

FireLine, 6 lb

Beading needle, size 12

Scissors

Chain-nose pliers

DIMENSIONS

8¼ x ⅝ inches (21 x 1.6 cm), not including clasp

the next 11°. String one drop bead, skip the "middle" 11° there, and weave through the following 11° (from step 3), the following bicone, and the next 11°. Repeat the last part of the step one time to add a third drop. If the center is still a bit loose, weave a second time through the beads of the last round (figure 5).

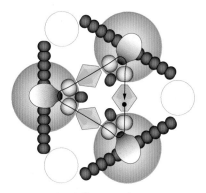

figure 5

6 Weave back to one of the arcs created in step 2. Counting from the middle 11° bead there, weave forward through the next two 15°s and exit. String one 15°, one 11°, and one 15°, and weave through the two 15°s, one 11°, and two 15°s in the middle of the next arc. Repeat two times to complete the round (figure 6).

The first component is done. Weave forward and exit from an 8-mm round bead.

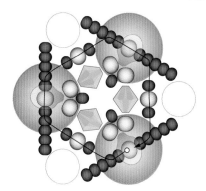

figure 6

7 Starting from the 8-mm round bead, make another ring as in step 1, stringing one 4-mm, one 8-mm, one 4-mm, one 8-mm, and one 4-mm round bead and weaving again through the 8-mm round bead where you started. This is the base for your next component. From here, repeat steps 2 through 6 (figure 7).

Once you finished the second component, weave along the pair of arcs above the 8-mm round bead connecting the two components. Exiting from a 15° at one end of an arc, string one 11° and enter the second arc. Repeat on the other side of the round bead (figure 7, red path and red outlines).

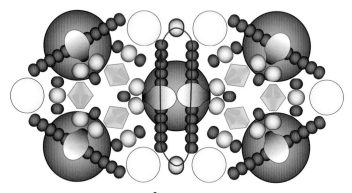

figure 7

8 After finishing the second component, continue making a strip by starting the next component from the second 4-mm round bead added in step 7. Include this 4-mm bead in your base row and embellish this component as described in steps 2 through 6.

Once this next component is finished, attach the arcs around this 4-mm bead, which is now linking components two and three. Following the red path in figure 8, and starting from the 11° added in step 6, weave through the following 15°, then weave into the last three 15°s of the arc above the 8-mm bead. String one 11° (figure 8, top red

outlines) and weave into the first three 15°s of the arc above the next 8-mm bead on the adjacent component. Weave into the 15°, 11°, and 15° of step 6, and from there into the last three 15°s of the arc above the next 8-mm bead. String one 11° (figure 8, bottom red outlines) and weave through the following three 15°s. The two components are connected now. Continue from the 8-mm round bead that is across from the 4-mm round bead where you started this component.

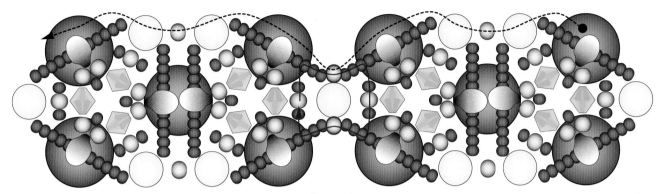

figure 8

9 Make one component after the other, alternating the starting point for each between an 8-mm bead and a 4-mm bead, until the bracelet reaches the desired length. Start and end the bracelet with a 4-mm round bead.

10 Make a loop to add to each end of the bracelet. Exit from the 15° before the 4-mm round bead. String two 15°s, one 11°, and two 15°s, skip the round bead, and weave into the first three 15°s after it. Weave along the three beads that correspond to those made in step 6 (15°, 11°, and 15°) and into the last three 15°s of the arc (you will exit where you started). If possible, weave a second time through the beads of this circuit. Exit from the newly added 11°. String five 11° seed beads and weave again through the 11° where you started and a second time through the beads of the loop. Finally, weave again through the beads of the loop and add a 15° bead in the second, third, fourth, and fifth gaps (figure 9).

11 After finishing the entire bracelet, weave along the beads on the outside edges. You can skip this step, however, if the tension in your beadwork is so high that this step is difficult.

Refer to the broken black line in figure 8. Starting from the 8-mm bead, weave through the following 4-mm bead, then through the 11° added in step 7, the next 8-mm bead, and the next 4-mm round bead. Weave through the 11° added in step 8 and the 4-mm and 8-mm beads. This step pulls the 11°s of steps 7 and 8 a bit down in between the round beads.

Finish

Mount the jump rings to the loops and attach the clasp.

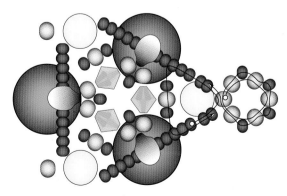

figure 9

SUPPLIES

6 rivolis, 8 mm (SS39), lilac

72 bicones, 3 mm, mint alabaster 2AB

7 g seed beads, 11°, matte brown

4 g seed beads, 11°, gold-violet

2 g seed beads, 15°, brown

2 g seed beads, 15°, gold

2 jump rings, 5 mm, 16 gauge, gold color

1 magnetic clasp

FireLine, 6 lb

Scissors

Chain-nose pliers

DIMENSIONS

6⅞ x ⅝ inches (17.5 x 1.6 cm) not including clasp

A FINE ROMANCE BRACELET

This bracelet uses a "fast" right angle weave stitch, where you string beads in just one direction. The procedure is to first make a base using this fast stitch, then create bridges over that base and connect them with bezeled rivolis. The number of rows in the base must be divisible by 8, and then add three (11, 19, 27, etc.).

1 Use only brown 15° and 11° seed beads for the base. Leave a 12-inch (30.5 cm) tail of thread to finish the bracelet after you make the base.

Following figure 1, string four 11°s to make a right angle weave unit. Continue in right angle weave to make a strip by adding five units to the first unit. Exit from the first bead on the edge, illustrated by the broken red path in figure 1.

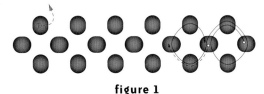

figure 1

2 String three 11° seed beads and weave again through the 11° you exited in step 1, then string one 15° and weave forward into the 11° that follows (figure 2).

figure 2

String two 11°s and weave through the next 11° from the previous unit, and then the 11° where you exited. String one 15° and weave forward into the next 11° of the strip. Repeat in this manner until reaching the end of the row (figure 3). Then continue making these rows in the same way until this base of the bracelet reaches the desired length—51 rows in this case (48 plus three).

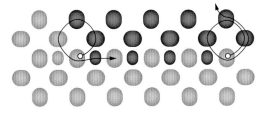

figure 3

3 Roll up the ends and zip the last row (row 51 is outlined in green in figure 4) to the one that is two rows before it (row 49 is outlined in red in figure 4). To do so, exit from a bead of row 51, heading toward the beadwork (not the outside), string one 11°, and weave in a circle through the matching bead of row 49. String another 11° and weave again through the bead where you started.

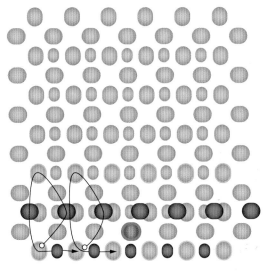

figure 4

Next, string one brown 15° and weave through the next 11° of row 51. As you did previously in this step, string one brown 11° and weave through the corresponding 11° bead in row 49, through the next 11° added to start this step, and then through the 11° where you started this portion of the step.

Again string a 15° and weave through the following size 11° of row 51. Repeat in this manner until the whole end is zipped.

4 Now make a loop, starting from the vertical bead in the middle of the bracelet's end (figure 4, purple outline). Exit from this bead, string five 11°s, and weave again through the bead where you exited. Weave a second time through the beads of the loop, and then weave along again for a third time, adding a 15° in the second, third, fourth, and fifth gaps between the 11°s.

Repeat this step on the other end of the bracelet.

5 Now it is time to make an embellishment between two 11° beads on each edge of the bracelet. Use only golden seed beads from this point on.

Following figure 5, exit from the 11° in the fourth row on one of the outside edges of the bracelet (the zipping row does not count, but the rows in the rolled part do!). String three golden 11° beads. Weave again through the bead where you exited, then weave forward and exit from the second golden bead just added. String one golden 15°, one 11°, one bicone, another 11°,

and one 15° before weaving again through the size 11° where you just exited. Weave forward and exit from the bicone bead.

String three bicones and weave again through the first bicone where you exited, exiting this time from the second of the three newly added bicones.

Continuing to reference figure 5, string one 11°, one 15°, one 11°, one 15°, and one 11° and weave again through the bicone just exited, then follow through the next 11° and 15° to exit from the second 11° just added. Finish this step by stringing one 11°, weaving through the 11° in this same row on the other edge, and stringing one 11° before weaving again through the 11° where you exited. This creates a link of right angle weave units between both edges.

6 Exiting from the 11° bead as illustrated in figure 6, fill the gaps along the edge of that link (black outlines in figure 6). Add one golden 11° bead in the following gap in front of the 15°, in each of the gaps before and after the next bicone, and in the gap after the next 15°. Repeat this on the other side of the link (figure 6).

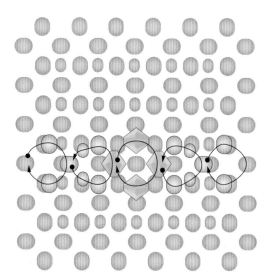

figure 5

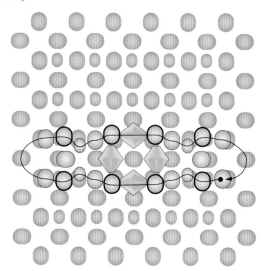

figure 6

7 Exit from an 11° in front of a bicone. String one 15°, one 11°, and one 15°, skip the bicone, and weave through the following 11° (figure 7). Repeat this on the other edge of the link.

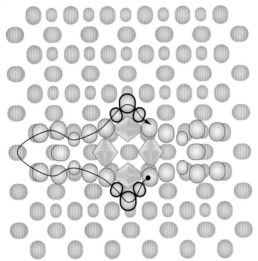

figure 7

8 Starting from the eighth row, make a second link by repeating steps 5 through 7 (there are three rows in the base between two links). Once finished, connect the second link to the first one with a bezeled rivoli.

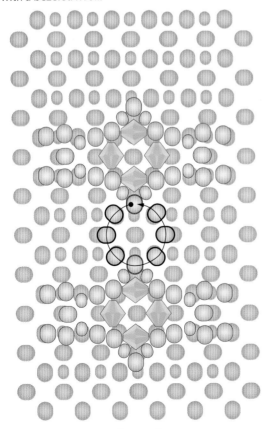

figure 8

To do this, exit from the size 11° above the bicone (added in the last row along the link, red outline in figure 8). String three 11° beads and weave through the corresponding 11° above the bicone of the previous link (figure 8, black outlines). String three more 11°s and weave again through all of the beads of this ring to tighten the thread and exit from the bead where you started the step.

9 String three 15°s, one 11°, and three 15°s, then weave again through the bead where you exited, creating a loop on top of it. Weave forward through the first 11° added in step 8 to the second bead added in that step. Make a similar loop there, and repeat two more times to make a total of four loops, as shown in figure 9, at the first, third, fifth, and seventh beads of the ring. To complete this step, weave through the last (eighth) 11° of the loop and into the 11° at the base of the first loop.

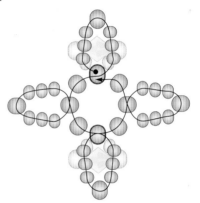

figure 9

10 Referring to figure 10, continue by weaving along the seven beads of the first loop, then—changing beading direction here—forward through the last (eighth) 11° bead of the connecting ring formed in step 8. From there, weave along the

figure 10

seven beads of the next loop. Continue in this manner around the loops of the ring. These loops become arcs, connected to the other 11°s of the ring.

11 The 11°s at the tips of each loop are outlined in green in both figures 10 and 11. Exit from one of these outlined beads and string two 15°s, one bicone, and two more 15°s. Weave through the 11° on the tip of the following loop. Repeat three times to complete going around. Place a rivoli into this bezel, front side up, and weave another time through the beads the ring just formed, but this time skip the green-outlined corner 11°s (figure 11). Weave at least one more time through these beads to secure the thread.

Note: It is important on this bezel to create strong tension, or the rivoli may pop out.

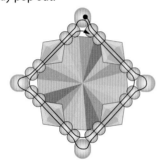

figure 11

12 Connect the outward-pointing 11° beads that form the tips of the rivoli bezel to the edges of the bracelet with right angle weave units. To make these units, exit from one of the 11° bezel tips and string one new 11°, then weave through the brown 11° on the edge of the base. Following the black path in figure 12, continue by stringing another 11° and weave again through the bead where you exited. Weave a second time through these four beads and then repeat this on the opposite tip pointing to the other edge.

One of the embellishments is now completed. Skip three rows in the base and start the next embellishment component on the fourth row. Create a total of six such components on the bracelet.

Finish

Mount the clasp with the jump rings at both ends to the bracelet. If you want to make the bracelet longer, either add rows in between the components or add more rows at the beginning and the end.

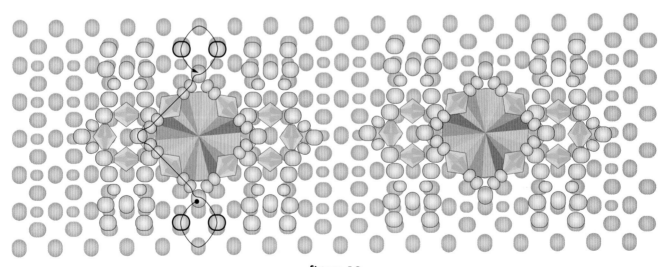

figure 12

AUNT LENI'S EARRINGS

This pair of earrings is actually a variation of Aunt Leni's Bracelet, which is found begining on page 65. Use cylinder beads in certain positions as indicated since the base has to be built so it is fairly stiff.

SUPPLIES

2 chatons, 8 mm, erinite

2 bicones, 4 mm, antique pink

8 bicones, 3 mm, erinite AB

4 round beads, 4 mm, jade

12 round beads, 3 mm, jade

1 g seed beads, 11°, iris gold

1 g seed beads, 15°, light gold

1 g cylinder beads, 11°, metallic rose

2 ear wires, gold

FireLine, 0.12 mm, 6 lb, smoke

Beading needle, size 12

Scissors

Chain-nose pliers

DIMENSIONS

1¾ x ½ inches (4.4 x 1.3 cm)

1 String four 11° seed beads and make a ring. Weave a second time through the four to secure the thread. Then create a loop by stringing five more 11° seed beads and weaving again through the bead where you exited. Weave again through the beads of the loop, then a third time, but this time add a 15° seed bead in the second, third, fourth, and fifth gaps between beads of the loop. Weave forward and exit from the bead in the original unit that is directly opposite the loop. Add one more unit in right angle weave using three 11° seed beads (figure 1, black path on far right).

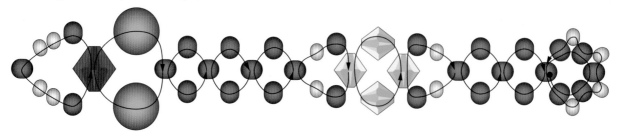

figure 1

Moving left in figure 1, continue with the next unit by stringing one 15° seed bead, one 11° seed bead, one 3-mm bicone, one 11° seed bead, and one more 15°. Weave again through the 11° where you started. Continue forward to exit from the bicone. String three more 3-mm bicones and weave again through the one where you exited. Weave forward and exit from the second bicone just added.

Continuing to follow figure 1 to the left, now string one 11° seed bead, one 15°, one 11° seed bead, one 15°, and one 11° seed bead for the next unit. Weave again through the bicone and exit from the second 11° just added. Add three more right angle weave units using 11° seed beads.

Starting from this point, string one 4-mm round bead, one 4-mm bicone, and another 4-mm round bead, and weave again through the 11° where you exited. Weave forward and exit from the bicone. String one 11° seed bead, two 15°s, another 11°, two more 15°s, and one 11° and weave again through the bicone. Weave once more through the beads of the last unit and exit from the 11° seed bead in front of the bicone.

2 Following the path in figure 2, add a 3-mm round bead and continue to weave all the way around the outside of the strip. As you go, add an 11° seed bead in the gap after the 4-mm round bead, a cylinder bead in each of the next two gaps, an 11° seed bead in each of the next four gaps, and a cylinder in the next gap.

Weave through the beads of the first unit you made in step 1, skipping the loop, and repeat adding beads in a mirror-image sequence, ending with a 3-mm round bead after the 4-mm round. Then continue to weave through and exit from the first round bead added in this step.

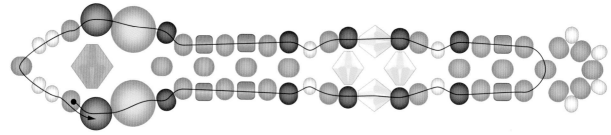

figure 2

3 Next add one 11° seed bead and four 15°s above the 4-mm round bead. Continue weaving around the outside edge and exit in front of the 3-mm bicone. Add one 15°, one 11° seed bead, and one 15°, then skip the 3-mm bicone and weave further along the outside of the strip. Follow figure 3 and add beads on the opposite edge of the strip in a mirror-image sequence, skipping the 11° seed bead at the tip to shape it.

Weave again through the beads of the entire perimeter to both secure the thread and stiffen the beaded strip, again skipping the 11° alone at the end opposite the loop to make an even sharper tip. Exit from one of the 11° seed beads outlined in faded red in figure 3.

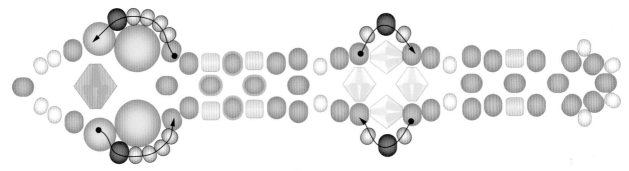

figure 3

4 Refer to steps 4 through 8 in Aunt Leni's Bracelet (pages 67-68) to add a chaton to the strip you have made in the first three steps.

Finish

Make a second earring like the first and mount the ear wires to the loops at the top of the strips.

III: Beaded Components and the Right Connections

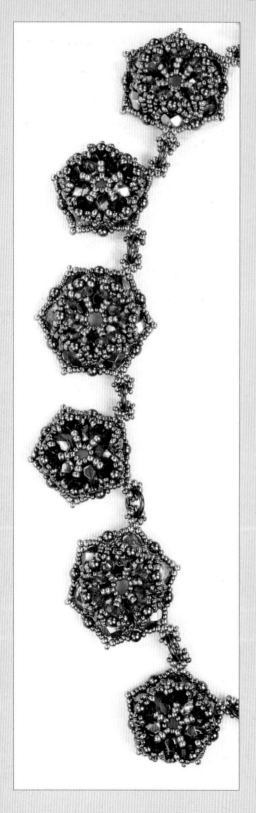

It can be difficult to arrange beaded parts in a way that they lie nicely around your neck or wrist. Jump rings can be attractive as well as functional for attaching beaded components in a flexible method, and clasps can often contribute to the beauty of a piece.

SUPPLIES

9 chatons, 8 mm, antique pink

12 bicones, 4 mm, rosaline

20 bicones, 3 mm, rosaline

24 round beads, 4 mm, platinum color

80 round beads, 3 mm, platinum color

8 g seed beads, 11°, pewter

3 g seed beads, 15°, light gold

Three-strand magnetic clasp, loops in a horizontal position

FireLine, 0.12 mm, 6 lb, smoke

Beading needle, size 12

Scissors

DIMENSIONS

6½ inches (16.5 cm) not including clasp

AUNT LENI'S BRACELET

Aunt Leni's bracelet consists of three strands. The outside ones are the same, while the design of the middle strand differs. The foundation of this bracelet is a beaded section made of nine right angle weave units. Three such sections complete one strand of the bracelet.

1 Starting with the first section of strand one, string three 11° seed beads and weave through the first loop of the clasp. Weave another time through the three beads and the loop to make a right angle weave unit (the loop counts as one bead).

Note: If you want the ability to adjust the length later, use an 11° seed bead here instead of attaching to the loop of the clasp.

Following the bead pattern in figure 1, exit from the 11° bead directly opposite from the loop. Stitch three more units in right angle weave using 11° beads. For the next portion of this section (the center segment), string one 15° seed bead, one 11° bead, one 3-mm bicone, one 11°, and one 15°. Weave again through the 11° where you exited to start this section, and then exit from the bicone. String one 3-mm round bead, one 3-mm bicone, and one 3-mm round bead, and weave again through the first bicone strung. Then weave forward and exit from the second bicone.

To complete the center segment, string one 11°, one 15°, one 11°, one 15°, and one 11° and weave again through the second bicone, exiting from the second 11° seed bead just added.

Now add another five right angle weave units using 11° seed beads.

Next in sequence is the end segment of this section (not the end of the bracelet, just the end of this section!). Exiting from the 11° at the end of the strand so far, string one 4-mm round bead, one 4-mm bicone, and one 4-mm round bead, weave again through the 11° where you exited, then weave for-ward and exit from the bicone bead. Finally for this section, string one 11°, two 15°s, one 11°, two 15°s, and one 11° and weave again through the bicone (figure 1).

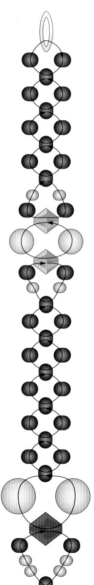

figure 1

2 Exiting from the 11° bead in front of the 4-mm bicone, weave along the outside edge of the strand after adding one 3-mm round bead in the gap next to the 4-mm bicone. Continue and add an 11° in all the other gaps (figure 2, dark seed beads); however, do not add a bead between the pairs of 15°s and 11°s next to the 3-mm bicones. At the end of the strand, weave through the clasp loop (no beads are added here) and similarly fill the gaps along the opposite edge with 11° beads. To fin-ish this step, add another 3-mm round bead next to the 4-mm bicone bead (figure 2).

figure 2

3 Weave another time along the outside edge, starting from the first 3-mm round bead added in step 2. String one 11° and four 15°s, skip the 4-mm round bead, and weave along the following beads before exiting before the 3-mm round bead. String four 15°s and skip the round bead. Weave along the strand to the other edge, repeating in a mirror-image sequence. Form a sharp tip at the end of the strand by skipping the 11° bead added in step 1 at the end of this strand (figure 3).

4 From the middle right angle weave unit of this base strand's end segment (figure 3, red outlines), start a chaton bezel by exiting from one of these 11° beads. String three 11°s and weave again through the seed bead where you exited. Weave forward to the next 11° of the base and repeat another three times before exiting from the middle 11° bead of the last unit (figure 4).

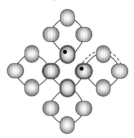

figure 4

5 String one 15° bead, one 3-mm round bead, and one 15°, and weave through the middle 11° bead of the next unit added in step 4. Repeat another three times to complete the circle and exit from the 11° bead that started this step (figure 5).

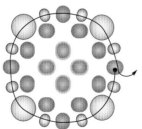

figure 5

6 String three 11°s and weave again through the 11° bead where you exited. Weave forward to the next 11° in the circle. Repeat three times and exit from a 3-mm round bead (figure 6).

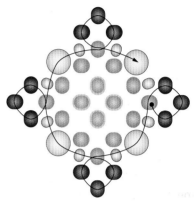

figure 6

7 Following figure 7, string one 15° bead and weave through the following three 11° beads added in step 6. String one 15° and weave through the following 3-mm round bead. Repeat three times to complete the circle. Continue forward to exit from the middle of three 11° seed beads added in step 6 (figure 7, broken path—the middle 11° beads are outlined as faded red in the figure).

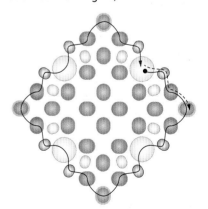

figure 7

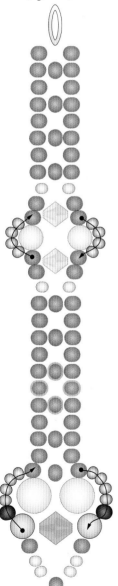

figure 3

8 String five 15° seed beads and weave through the middle bead in the next group of three 11°s (figure 8, red outlines). Repeat three times to complete going around. Loosen the thread, then place a chaton into the cup, front side up. Pull the thread again and weave another time through the beads of this circuit to secure the thread. Now weave a third time through the beads in this step, but this time skip the 11°s in the corners (figure 8).

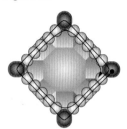

figure 8

9 Weave back to the base and exit from the 11° bead that is the tip of the end segment (figure 9, faded blue outline near top).

At this point, extend the strand by stringing two 15° beads, one 11°, one 4-mm bicone, another 11°, and two 15°s. Weave again through the 11° where you started and then forward to the bicone just added. String one 4-mm round bead, one 11° bead, and one 4-mm round bead, then weave through the beads and exit from the last 11° added.

Add five right angle weave units using only 11° beads, followed by a center segment as made in step 1. Add five more right angle weave units using 11° beads, and finish by making an end segment, again as made in step 1.

Embellish the strand's extension by adding round beads and 11° seed beads (figure 9, green outlines) as described in steps 2 and 3. Add a chaton bezel (as described in steps 4 through 8) at the middle unit of both five-unit right angle weave sections just stitched (figure 9, red outlines). Take care that all bezels are on the front side of the bracelet.

10 Starting from the 11° at the tip of the segment's unattached end, continue the strand by making a section that is a mirror-image version of that made in steps 1 through 8. Attach it to the corresponding loop of the other half of the clasp.

11 Repeat steps 1 through 10 to make another strand and attach it to the third position of the clasp, leaving the set of middle loops free.

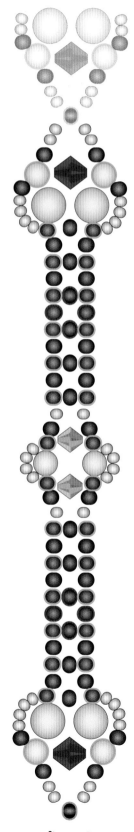

figure 9

12 The third strand, for the middle position in the bracelet, is designed a bit differently than the first two. Referring to figure 10, start from the clasp and make a right angle weave unit of 11° beads (including the loop of the clasp). Add two more right angle weave units using 11°s. Add one center segment, then three more right angle weave units using 11°s, another center segment, three more right angle weave 11° units, and finally one end segment (as described in step 1). Add round beads and 11° beads to embellish the outside edges (figure 10, green outlines), as done at the end of step 9.

13 Starting from the 11° bead at the tip of the section completed in the previous step, make one end segment, then seven right angle weave units using 11°s, and another end segment. Embellish along the edges as shown in the previous sections (figure 11, green outlines) and make one chaton bezel in the middle right angle weave unit of this section (figure 11, red outlines).

14 To finish this strand, make a mirror-image version of the segment made in step 12.

Finish

If you ended the strands with a seed bead instead of attaching to the loops of the clasp, you can lengthen the bracelet either by adding beaded loops or sewing the ends to another type of clasp. Especially when the loops of the clasp are in a vertical position, you cannot simply attach them to the beadwork without twisting. A beaded loop in the end and then a link with a jump ring might be helpful to solve the problem.

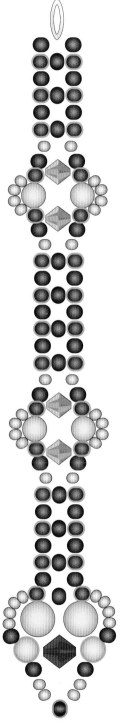

figure 10

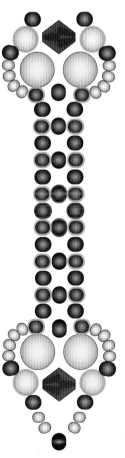

figure 11

This is the underside of Aunt Leni's Bracelet

BEADED CHARMS BRACELET

Who said a charm cannot be beaded; and who said a chain has to be metal?

Check out this playful bracelet!

Make the Charms

1 String one 11° seed bead, one 3.4-mm drop bead, one more 11°, and one rizo bead. Repeat four times, making a ring, and then weave again through all the beads (figure 1).

figure 1

2 Exit from an 11° and string an 8-mm round bead, positioning it in the center of your ring. Weave through the 11° directly opposite the 11° you exited, and then back through the round bead and into the first 11° again (figure 2).

figure 2

3 The next step is to weave along the beads of the ring surrounding the round bead and stitch a right angle weave unit at each 3.4-mm drop bead and rizo bead. To do this, weave forward and exit from a drop bead. String one 15°, one 11°, and one 15°, then weave again through the drop. The added beads will be positioned underneath the drop. Then weave forward through the size 11° and the rizo bead. String one 15°, one 11°, and one 15°, and weave again through the rizo bead. These newly added beads will be positioned on top. Repeat alternating to finish around the ring. Figure 3 shows the beadwork from the side.

figure 3

4 Exit from the 11° of the right angle weave unit at the first 3.4-mm drop bead strung in the previous step. String one 15°, one 11°, and one 15°, then

SUPPLIES

12 round beads, 8 mm, pearl white

12 round beads, 6 mm, pearl white

4 g rizo beads (long drop 2.5 x 5.5 mm), purple

4 g drop beads, 3.4 mm, aqua violet lined

6 g seed beads, 11°, dark bronze

3 g seed beads, 15°, blue-green metallic

14 jump rings, 5.5 mm, 16 gauge, silver

Magnetic clasp

FireLine, 0.12 mm, 6 lb

Beading needle, size 12

Scissors

Chain-nose pliers

DIMENSIONS

6¾ x 1¼ inches (17.1 x 3.2 cm), not including clasp

weave through the 11° of the right angle weave unit above the next drop bead. Repeat four times to complete the round. Weave another time through these beads to secure the thread (figure 4).

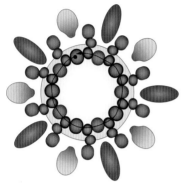

figure 4

5 Repeat step 4 on the other side of the round bead, but this time connect the 11°s above the rizo beads (figure 5).

figure 5

Repeat steps 1 through 5 to make a total of 12 charms, or components.

6 Make a loop for each charm. For six of them, exit from the 11° bead that started step 4, in position above the 3.4-mm drop bead. String five 11°s and weave again through the 11° where you exited. Weave once more through all the beads of this loop. Add a 15° bead in the second, third, fourth, and fifth gaps between the 11°s (figure 6, top).

Begin the loops for the remaining six charms from the 11° bead that started step 5, in position above the rizo bead. Once more string five 11°s and weave again through the 11° where you exited. Weave another time through all the beads of this loop and add a 15° bead in the second, third, fourth, and fifth gaps between the 11°s (figure 6, bottom).

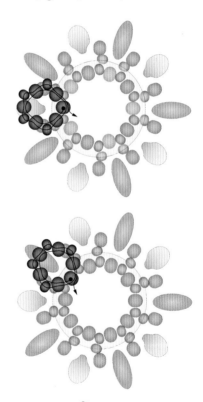

figure 6

Make the Base

7 To start the base on which the charms will be mounted, make a right angle weave unit from four 11° seed beads, then add one loop (like those illustrated in step 6) to one of the 11°s in the new unit. Exit from the 11° positioned directly opposite the loop (figure 7).

figure 7

8 String one 11°, one 6-mm round bead, and three 11°s, and weave back through the round bead. String another 11° and weave again through the 11° where you started. Continue by weaving forward (figure 8, broken path) and exit from the second 11° on the other side of the round bead.

String one 3.4-mm drop bead, one 11°, and one more drop bead before weaving again through the 11° where you exited. Weave forward and exit from the newly added 11°.

Repeat this step 10 times. After adding the 12th round bead, make a right angle weave unit using only 11° beads (no 3.4-mm drops beads) and add one loop at the other end of the strip (figure 8).

9 Weave along the outside edge, adding one 11° after the first 11° bead. Weave through the next 11° and exit before the round bead.

String two 15°s, three 11°s , and two 15°s. Skip the round bead and weave through the following 11°. String one 11° and weave through the 3.4-mm drop bead. Continue by stringing an 11° and weaving through the following 11°, exit before the round bead.

Repeat the stringing pattern just described until you reach one end of the base. At that point, add one 11° in the gap between the two 11°s there. Repeat along the opposite edge of the base (figure 9).

10 Make 12 loops like those in step 6 and add one to each of the middle 11°s above the round beads, all on the same edge of the bracelet (figure 10).

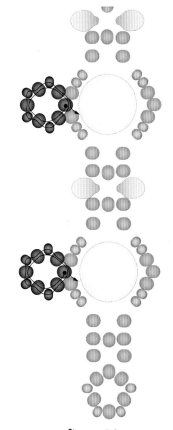

figure 10

Finish

Mount the charms to the loops of the bracelet using jump rings. Make sure the loops are all pointing to the back and the two different charms are mounted in an alternating sequence. Add the clasp to the loops at the beginning and the end of the base.

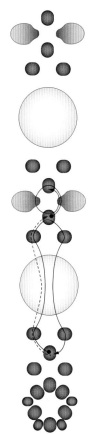

figure 8

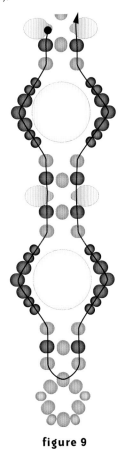

figure 9

SUPPLIES

14 round beads, 8 mm, jade color

77 round beads, 4 mm, jade color

112 bicones, 3 mm, blue zircon 2AB

5 g seed beads, 11°, metallic blue-green

11 g seed beads, 11°, silver color

4 g seed beads, 15°, metallic blue

5 g seed beads, 15°, silver color

35 jump rings, 5.5 mm, 16 gauge

FireLine, 6 or 8 lb

Beading needle, size 12

Scissors

Chain-nose pliers

DIMENSIONS

38.5 inches (97.8 cm) long, not including clasp. The length can be easily modified by changing the number of the single elements.

OPPOSITES ATTRACT NECKLACE

The longer a necklace, the more its components tend to twist. Turn this to your advantage by making your components bilateral—with each side a different color—to produce a beautiful effect. This design allows single elements to be perfect earrings, too.

1 Make a bezel for an 8-mm round bead. To do so, string 24 blue 15° seed beads and make a base ring by weaving again through the first bead. Then weave forward through the beads of the entire ring to secure the thread.

String one 8-mm round bead and hold it in the center of the ring. Exit underneath the ring on the opposite side of the round bead (between the 12th and 13th seed beads as shown in figure 1), and go through the round bead again from above. In this way the beading thread is looped around the thread of the ring. Weave back to the other side of the round bead and through the 15° bead that is adjacent to the seed bead where you started.

figure 1

2 Add one row of blue 15°s using circular peyote stitch as follows: String one blue 15°, skip one bead in the base row, and weave through the next one in the base row. Repeat 11 times to complete the row, exiting from the first bead added (figure 2).

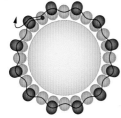

figure 2

3 Add two more rows in circular peyote stitch, this time using silver 11° seed beads. Step up at the end of the rows through the first bead added. In figure 3, the black path shows the first row and the red path shows the second row.

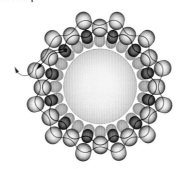

figure 3

4 Still weaving in circular peyote, make another row by adding two silver 15° seed beads in each gap. Exit after the first bead added (figure 4).

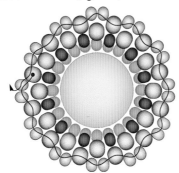

figure 4

5 Using only silver beads in this step, string one 11° and weave through the following 15°, 11°, and two 15°s. Continue by stringing one 15°, one 11°, and one 15°. Skip one 11° and weave through the following four beads (two 15°s, one 11°, one 15°).

Repeat the entire step three times (figure 5).

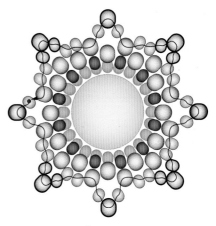

figure 5

6 Weave back through the beads to the first row and flip the beadwork over. Repeat steps 3 and 4 on the other side by using blue-green 11° and blue 15° beads instead of silver. Position these beads to correspond with the silver rows and sizes.

For the last (outer) row, weave through the following silver 11° from step 5 and also through the next four beads (one blue 15°, one blue-green 11°, and two blue 15°s). Continue by stringing one blue 15°, one blue-green 11°, and another blue 15° (figure 6, red outlines). Skip one 11° and weave through the following four beads (two blue 15°s, one

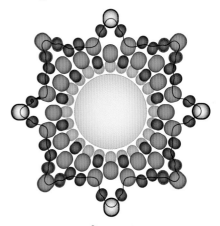

figure 6

blue-green 11°, and one blue 15°). Weave through the next silver 11° and repeat this pattern to complete going all the way around.

Weaving through the silver 11°s in this step connects the front and back layers of the bezel.

7 Start from one of the silver seed beads connecting the bezel layers (figure 7, black outlines) and string one bicone, one silver 11°, one 4-mm round bead, one silver 11°, and another bicone. Following the solid black path in figure 7, weave through the following silver 11° "connector." Repeat another three times to complete the row, then weave forward (figure 7, broken black path) and exit in front of another silver connector bead. This row lies around the outside edge of the bezel.

Following the red path in figure 7, string one silver 15°, one silver 11°, and one silver 15°. Skip the connector and weave through the following beads until you exit in front of the next connector. Repeat three times to complete going around.

8 Add a loop of silver beads to the bezel. Exit from one of the 11° beads added to the outside row in the previous step. String five 11°s, pass through the bead where you exited, and weave a second time through the beads of the loop. Add one 15° in the second, third, fourth, and fifth gaps (figure 8).

figure 7

figure 8

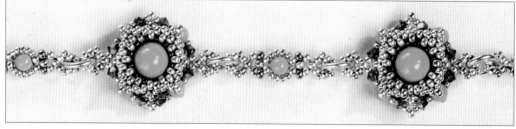

Repeat on the opposite side of the bezel unit to add a second loop. Secure the thread and cut it off.

9 Repeat steps 1 through 8 to make a total of 14 bezeled round beads.

10 Using silver seed beads throughout this step, make a link for connecting the bezeled elements. Start by stringing six 11° beads and weaving another time through them to make a loop. Weave a third time through, adding a 15° in the second, third, fourth, and fifth gaps (figure 9, black path). Exit from the 11° that has no adjacent 15° beads.

String three 11°s and weave again through the bead where you just exited. Continue to weave forward and exit from the second 11° just added (figure 9, green path).

String one 11° bead, one 4-mm round bead, and three 11°s, and weave back through the round bead. String one 11° and weave again through the 11° bead where you started this portion of the step (figure 9, solid red path).

Weave along the next 11°, round bead, and 11°, and exit from the second 11° after the round bead (figure 9, broken red path). From here, mirror the elements at the beginning of the link by adding a group of three 11° beads followed by another loop of 11°s with 15° beads in the gaps. Exit from the 11° bead that starts this last loop.

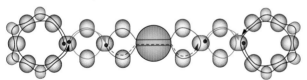

figure 9

11 Follow the path shown in figure 10 to weave along the edge of the link, but not through the loops at either end. Add one blue-green 11° bead in the first gap as shown. Continue weaving along, skipping the round bead but adding four silver 15° beads above it. Add one more blue-green 11° in the following gap. Repeat on the opposite edge of the link. Weave several times along the beads of the last row to secure the thread.

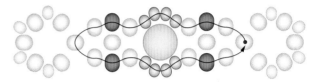

figure 10

12 Repeat steps 10 and 11 to make additional links. Make a total of 19 links as described above, and make two additional links switching blue-green and silver beads.

Finish

Connect all the separate components to each other by attaching jump rings through all the loops. I created the necklace shown here by connecting the elements in an asymmetrical series as follows (all bezeled round beads face with the silver side showing unless otherwise indicated): one silver link, one blue-green link, eight silver links, one blue-green bezeled round bead, one silver link, one blue-green link, one silver link, one bezeled round bead, one silver link, one bezeled round bead, one silver link, one bezeled round bead, one silver link, three bezeled round beads, one silver link, one bezeled round bead, one silver link, one bezeled round bead, one blue-green bezeled round bead, one bezeled round bead, and finally one silver link and one bezeled round bead, three times alternating.

HOKKAIDO FLOWERS NECKLACE

This piece of beadwork is made from alternating hexagonal and pentagonal components. Hexagons are prefect structures to maintain a straight shape, like a bracelet. Pentagons invite an arc formation. Combined here, they create a gentle curve to drape around your neck.

Hexagon

1 Following figure 1, string one fire-polished bead, one 11° bead, one fire-polished, two 11°s, another fire-polished, and two more 11°s. Weave again through the first fire-polished bead to create a ring. Weave a second time through all the beads and exit from the second fire-polished bead.

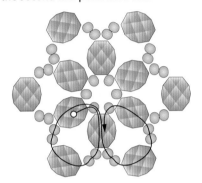

figure 1

2 Still referring to figure 1, string two 11°s, one fire-polished bead, two more 11°s, a fire-polished bead, and another 11°, then again weave through the fire-polished bead where you exited. Weave forward and exit from the last fire-polished bead just added.

Continue by stringing one 11°, one fire-polished bead, two 11°s, another fire-polished, and two more 11°s and weave again through the fire-polished bead where you just exited. Weave forward and exit from the first fire-polished bead just added.

3 Repeat step 2. This gives a strip of five units that are starting to form a curve. Make a circle from these units with the thread exiting from the fire-polished bead at the end of the strip. String two 11°s, one fire-polished

bead, and two more 11°s, then weave through the fire-polished bead of the first unit. String one 11° and weave again through the fire-polished bead where you last exited.

4 Exit from an 11° bead in the center of the circle. String one 15° bead and weave through the following 11° in the circle. Repeat five times to complete the step. Exit from the 11° where the step started (figure 2).

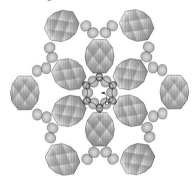

figure 2

A framework of six units for the hexagon has been completed. All six units will be embellished separately in the same way.

5 Exiting from an 11° bead in the center, string two 11°s, one green bicone, one 11°, and three 15°s, skip the fire-polished bead of the same unit, and weave through the first of the next two consecutive 11°s. Then string three 15°s, one 11°, one round bead, one more 11°, and three 15°s. Skip the following 11° bead (the second of a set of two), the fire-polished bead, and the first of a pair of 11°s in the same unit, and continue by weaving through the following 11° (the second of a set of two). String three 15°s, one 11°, and one green bicone. Weave through the first pair of 11°s added in

SUPPLIES

164 fire-polished beads, 6 mm, metallic green violet

84 bicones, 3 mm, erinite (light blue green)

80 bicones, 3 mm, amethyst

164 round beads, 3 mm, hot pink

14 g seed beads, 11°, metallic light green

10 g seed beads, 15°, metallic rose

16 jump rings, 5 mm, 16 gauge, black

1 toggle clasp, black

FireLine, 0.12 mm, 6 lb, smoke

Beading needle, size 12

Scissors

Chain-nose pliers

DIMENSIONS

19¼ x 1 inches (48.9 x 2.5 cm) not including clasp

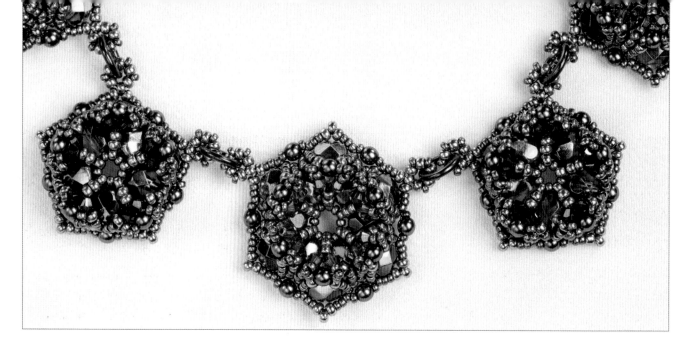

this step, heading to the middle of the hexagon. Weave again in the same direction through the 11° where you started (figure 3).

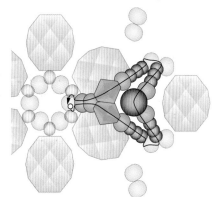

figure 3

6 Exit from the first bicone added in step 3 and continue weaving through the round bead of the following arc and the second bicone added. These three beads form a triangle on top of the component. Weave another time along these three beads, but this time add three 15° beads before and three after the round bead. Shape each group of three 15°s into a picot (figure 4).

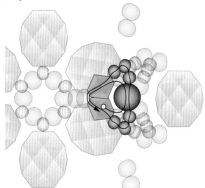

figure 4

Weave forward to the next 11° in the center of the component and repeat steps 5 and 6 here and on the following four units.

7 Weave along the outside edge. There are sets of four 11°s between each of the fire-polished beads. Weave along one of the sets and exit in front of the fire-polished bead. String three 15° beads, two 11°s, and three 15°s, then skip the fire-polished bead and weave through the following four 11°s.

Repeat this step five times and exit in the middle of the first arc created in this step, between the pair of 11°s (figure 5).

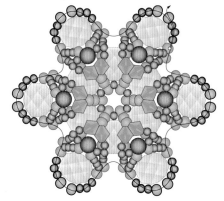

figure 5

8 Again weave along the outside edge. String one 11° and weave through the following four beads (one 11° and three 15°s). Then string a 15°, a round bead, and another 15° before skipping the four 11°s that follow, and continue to weave through the next four beads (three 15°s and one 11°).

Repeat the step five times (figure 6).

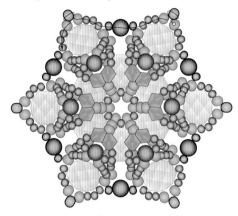

figure 6

9 Make a loop by starting from the 11° bead at one tip of the hexagonal component, string five more 11°s, and weave again through the 11° where you exited. Weave another time through the beads of the loop to tighten the thread. Then weave a third time through that loop and add a 15° bead in the second, third, fourth, and fifth gaps between the 11°s (figure 7).

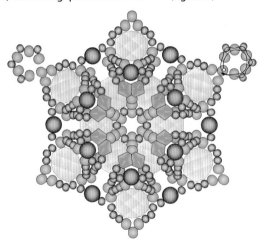

figure 7

Skip one tip of the hexagon and make another loop at the next one.

Make a pentagonal component by following steps 1 through 8, but make these alterations:

1. Following the first three steps, make four units before closing the circle with the fifth instead of the sixth.

2. In step 5, use amethyst-colored bicones instead of the green ones. You will see that the center of this component will appear like a little plateau, instead of the deepening of the hexagonal shape.

3. Make loops on two adjacent tips in step 9.

Finish

Make a total of eight pentagonal and seven hexagonal components. Start with a pentagon and mount a hexagonal next to it by attaching the loops with a jump ring. Alternate pentagons and hexagons, ending with a pentagon. Mount the toggle clasp at each end of the necklace with jump rings.

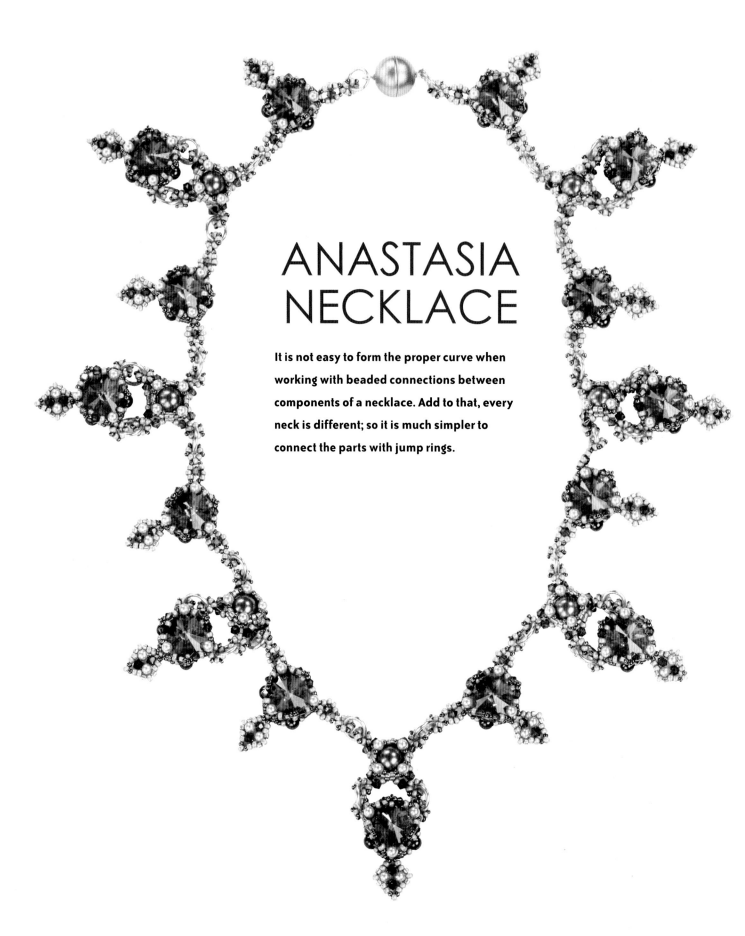

ANASTASIA
NECKLACE

It is not easy to form the proper curve when working with beaded connections between components of a necklace. Add to that, every neck is different; so it is much simpler to connect the parts with jump rings.

Component One

1 String four cylinder beads and two size 15° seed beads, then repeat three times. Make a ring by weaving again through all 24 beads. Exit after the second cylinder in one of the rows (figure 1).

figure 1

2 String one 8-mm round bead and place it in the center of the ring. Exit from the round bead underneath the ring of beads and enter it again from above the ring so that the thread wraps around the ring. Let the thread slip in the gap between the second and third cylinder beads of the ring, and weave back through the round bead. Finish this step by weaving along the third and fourth cylinder beads on the side where you started (figure 2).

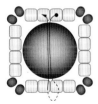

figure 2

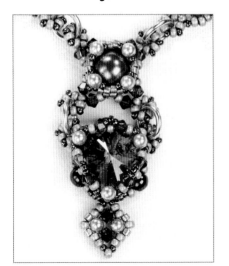

3 Following the solid black path in figure 3, continue weaving and exit between the next two 15°s. String one 15° and weave through the following 15° and the next cylinder bead. String two cylinder beads while skipping two from the original ring, then weave through the next cylinder. Repeat three times and exit from the first pair of cylinder beads added in this step (figure 3, broken black path).

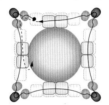

figure 3

4 String one 15°, one 3-mm round bead, and one 15°, skip the corner, and weave through the following pair of cylinder beads that was added in the previous step. Repeat three times to complete the circuit and weave a second time through the beads to secure the thread (figure 4).

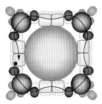

figure 4

SUPPLIES

15 rivolis, 14 mm, padparadscha

192 bicones, 3 mm, amethyst

7 round beads, 8 mm, copper color

45 round beads, 4 mm, dark purple

103 round beads, 3 mm, light peach

3 g cylinder beads, 11° light gold

11 g seed beads, 11°, matte light gold

6 g seed beads 15°, light bronze

30 jump rings 5.5 mm, 16 gauge, gold color

1 magnetic clasp, 14 mm

FireLine, 0.12 mm, 6 lb

Beading needle, size 12

Scissors

Chain-nose pliers

DIMENSIONS

19½ inches (49.5 cm) long, not including clasp

5 Weave forward through the beads and exit from the third of a four-cylinder sequence from step 1. Flip the beadwork and continue working from the back. String one 11° light gold seed bead, one bicone, one more 11° seed bead, one bicone, and another 11° seed bead, and weave through the two middle cylinder beads in the next group of four. Repeat three more times to complete the circuit and reinforce the entire round to secure the thread (figure 5).

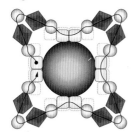

figure 5

6 Add a loop to one of the 11° seed beads in a corner. To do so, exit from one of the corner 11°s, string five 11° seed beads, weave again through the bead where you exited, and then weave a second time through the beads of the loop. Weave a third time along the loop and add a 15° seed bead in the second, third, fourth, and fifth gaps, as shown in figure 6. Repeat at the other 11° seed beads on each of the remaining three corners.

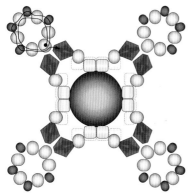

figure 6

Repeat steps 1 through 6 to make a total of seven components.

Component Two

7 String one 11° gold seed bead and six cylinder beads. Repeat two times and make a triangle-shaped ring by weaving again through the first 11° bead. Weave another two times through the beads of the ring and exit from an 11°. String one 15°, another 11° seed bead, and a 15° and weave again through the 11° bead where you exited (figure 7). Repeat this and add two more right angle weave units on the other two 11° beads of this ring. Exit from the 11° in the last unit added.

figure 7

8 String three 15°s, one 11° seed bead, one bicone, one 11°, one bicone, one 11°, and three 15°s, and weave through the 11° seed bead of the following right angle weave unit added in the previous step. Repeat two times to complete this circuit, making three circuits around the

triangle of step 7 (figure 8). Weave another time through these beads to secure the thread and exit from the first bicone added in this step.

figure 8

9 Place the rivoli into the cup and pull the three arcs on top of the rivoli, noting that it is not fully secure yet. String three 15°s, skipping the 11° between the bicones added in the previous step, and weave through the following bicone, the 11°, and the first of the following three consecutive 15°s. Push the three 15°s you just strung to form a picot. Continue by stringing a 3-mm round bead while skipping the five beads in the corner, and weave through the following 15°, 11°, and bicone. Repeat two times to complete this circuit (figure 9). Pull the thread

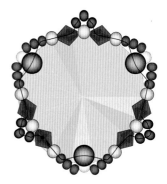

figure 9

carefully so as not to break it. The beads should be close together with no gaps, especially before and after the round beads. The rivoli is still not completely secured. Take care that it does not slip out of the bezel.

10 Flip the beadwork over and exit from the 11° seed bead where you started step 8. String three 15°s, one 11° seed bead, one 4-mm round bead, another 11°, and three 15°s. Weave through the 11° bead of the next right angle weave unit. Repeat two times to complete going around (figure 10). Weave another time through to secure the thread. The beads of this circuit secure the rivoli from the bottom. Exit from the 11° where you started this round.

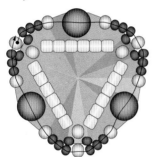

figure 10

11 As shown in figure 11, add a loop (see step 6, same as you did in Component One) to an 11° seed bead in two of the three corners that are the tips of the right angle weave units added in step 7. Exiting from the 11° at the third corner, string one 15°, one 11° seed bead, one bicone, another 11°, and one 15°, and weave again through the bead where you exited. Weave forward and exit from the bicone. String one 3-mm round bead, one bicone, and one 3-mm round bead, and weave again through the bicone where you started. Then weave forward and exit from the bicone just added. String one 11° seed bead, one 15°, one 11°, one 15°,

and one 11°, and weave again through the bicone. Weave along the beads of this last part and exit from an 11° in front of a bicone (figure 11).

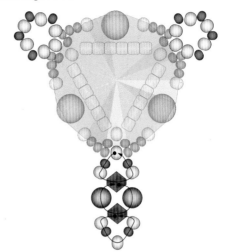

figure 11

12 Following the solid black path in figure 12, string one 11° seed bead and weave through the following round bead. String another 11° seed bead and weave through the following 11° and 15° seed beads. Skip the next 11° on the tip and weave through the following 15° and 11° seed beads. Add an 11° seed bead before and after the next round bead, then weave forward, skipping the 11° seed bead on the next tip, to the first 11° bead added in this step.

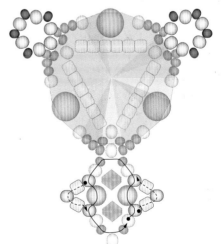

figure 12

Exit from the 11° in front of the round bead. String one 11° cylinder bead, one 11° seed bead, and one cylinder, skip the round bead, and weave through the following 11° seed bead (figure 12, broken black path). Weave forward along the beads and repeat this above the round bead on the other side of the strip. Secure the thread and tail and cut off.

Repeat steps 7 through 12 to make a total of seven Component Twos.

Component Three

13 Repeat steps 7 through 10. Then make a bottom tip on an 11° seed bead as described in steps 11 and 12. Instead of just adding the loops in the other two positions, you will bead little extensions. Exiting from the 11° in one of the corners, string one 15°, one 11° seed bead, one bicone, one 11°, and one 15°, and weave again through the bead where you exited, and then forward until you exit from the bicone. String one 11° seed bead, one 15°, one 11°, one 15°, and one 11°, and weave again through the bicone. Weave along the beads of this last portion and exit from an 11° bead in front of a bicone. String one 11° seed bead so it is in the gap between two 11°s, weave along the outside beads of this small extension to the other end of the bicone, and add one 11° seed bead in the gap here, as well (figure 13). Add one loop (again, same as step 6 in Component One) at the end of this extension (figure 14).

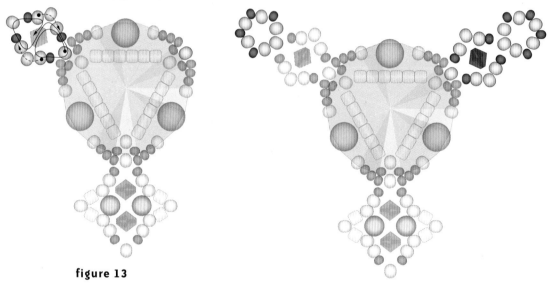

figure 13

figure 14

14 Repeat step 13 on the third (open) corner.

Repeat steps 13 and 14 to make a total of eight Component Threes.

Finish

Attach all Component Threes to Component Ones, alternating but starting and ending with Component Threes. Use jump rings in each of two loops in the seven Component Ones, leaving two loops (lower) empty. Then mount one Component Two to each of the empty loops on the Component Ones. Attach the magnetic clasp using jump rings at the first and the last Component Threes.

IV: Embellished Shapes and Shaped Embellishments

Embellishments not only add to the look of a beaded piece, they can be fundamental in forming and shaping the piece. An embellishment can make the difference between an amorphous design and a beautifully shaped piece of jewelry.

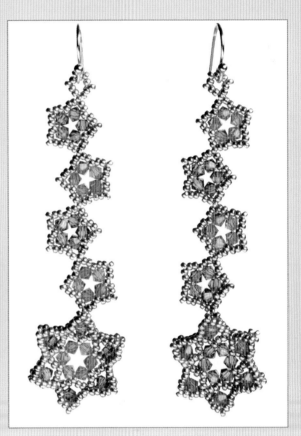

HELENA'S RING(S)

The dome shape gives this ring its eye-catching appeal from every viewing angle.

SUPPLIES

1 chaton, 8 mm, gold colored

4 chatons, 8 mm, vintage rose

24 bicones, 3 mm, amethyst 2AB

16 round beads, 3 mm, ancient rose

20 fire-polished beads, 4 mm, ancient rose

2 g double-hole beads (superduo or twin beads), green luster

5 g seed beads, 11°, metallic champagne

1 g seed beads, 15°, metallic yellow gold colored

FireLine, 6 or 8 lb

Beading needle, size 12

Scissors

DIMENSIONS

1¼ x 1¼ inches (3.2 x 3.2 cm)

1 Start with two wingspans of thread. Make a base in right angle weave using fire-polished beads. To do so, string four of them and make a ring by weaving again through the first one strung, as shown in the center section of figure 1. The tail as well as the working thread should each be one wingspan, with the strung beads in the middle of the thread. Weave through a second time to secure the thread, then weave a third time, adding one 11° bead after each fire-polished bead.

Exit from a fire-polished bead and string three more of the same. Weave again through the bead from which you exited. In this way, add one new unit of right angle weave on each of the four beads in the initial ring (figure 1).

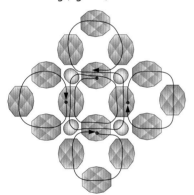

figure 1

2 From one of these new units, exit from a fire-polished bead that is adjacent to another ring, heading toward the outside, as shown in figure 2. String one fire-polished bead and weave through the fire-polished bead of the adjacent unit and through the one you exited from.

This makes a triangle. Weave another time through the beads of this triangle and add one 11° bead after each of the three fire-polished beads. Repeat this step in the other three corners of the base (figure 2).

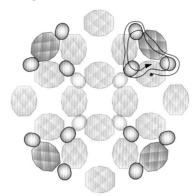

figure 2

3 Turn the beadwork over and continue working from the reverse side. Weave through the eight fire-polished beads on the outside edge of the base and add one 11° bead after each of them (figure 3). Weave twice through the circle to tighten the thread. The base will now form a cup. The 11°s added in steps 1 and 2 should be on the outside of this cup.

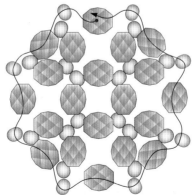

figure 3

4 Continue by working on the front side. In this step you will make arcs around each of the four fire-polished beads in the initial right angle weave unit (center of the base) created in step 1. Exit from one of the 11° beads that is in front of one of those fire-polished beads. String two 15° beads, one double-hole bead, and four 15°s. Stitch down through the second hole of the double-hole bead, string two more 15°s, and weave through the next 11° that is after the fire-polished bead. Repeat three more times to complete going around that middle unit. Weave through to exit from the second of the four 15° beads above the double-hole bead that was strung first (figure 4, black path).

String one 11° and weave through the next two 15°s. String two 11°s and weave through the two 15°s that are above the second double-hole bead. Repeat three more times to complete going around (figure 4, red path). Exit from the first 11° added in this step.

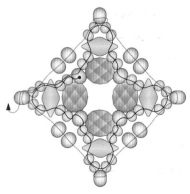

figure 4

5 String one 11°, one bicone, and one 11°. Weave through the following 11° above the next double-hole bead. Repeat three more times to complete going around.

Loosen the thread and put the gold-colored chaton into the cup. Pull the thread and weave another time through the beads around the chaton (figure 5, black path and outlines). Exit from the 11° from which you started this step.

String one 11°, one round bead, two 11°s, another round bead, and one 11°. Skip the next three beads that surround the chaton (11°, bicone, 11°) and weave through the following 11° bead (figure 5, red path and outlines). Repeat this three more times to complete going around, then exit between the first pair of consecutive 11°s strung for this row.

Following the green path in figure 5, string an 11° and weave through the following seven beads (11°, round, 11°, 11°, 11°, round, 11°). Repeat three times to complete going around.

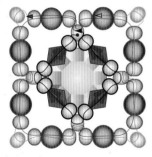

figure 5

6 Weave forward along the beads and exit from one of the three 11°s added when you made triangles in step 2. You are going to prepare a triangle-shaped bezel for each of the remaining four chatons.

As you did in step 4, make an arc on this triangle by stringing two 15°s, a double-hole bead, and four 15°s, and then stitch through the other opening in the double-hole bead before stringing two more 15°s. Go through the next 11° and make a second, identical arc. Repeat to make a third arc.

To make the next row, weave through to exit from the second 15° above the double-hole bead that was strung first in this step. String one 11° and weave through the following two 15°s. String three 11°s and weave through the first two 15°s that are above the second double-hole bead. Repeat two more times to complete going around (figure 6). Exit from one of the 11°s above a double-hole bead.

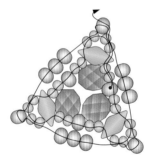

figure 6

7 To complete the bezel for one of the rose-colored chatons, string two 11° beads, one bicone, and two 11°s. Weave through the next 11° above the next double-hole bead. Repeat two more times and then weave a second time through the beads of this row. Push a rose chaton into the cup and let it slip underneath the beads of the triangle—knowing that it is not yet secure.

Exit in front of a bicone. String four 15° beads and weave through the following five 11°s. Repeat two more times (above each of the other two bicones) and exit after the second 15° in the first group of four just strung in this row.

As illustrated in figure 7, add one 11° bead in the middle of the two outside groups of 15° beads. In the position where the square bezel (from step 5) is adjacent to the new bezel, weave through the 11° on that corner. Take care to have strong tension in the last two rows to make sure the chaton is secure.

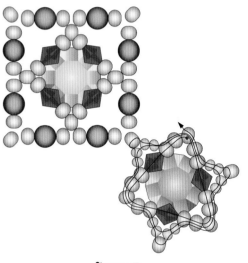

figure 7

8 Repeat steps 6 and 7 at the next corner of the square holding the gold-colored chaton to make a second triangular bezel. Now you will make a link to attach these two bezels.

Exit from the middle 11° bead on one of the edges of a bezel as shown in figure 8. String one 15°, one 11°, one bicone, one 11°, and one 15°. Weave again through the 11° from which you exited, then stitch forward and exit from the bicone. Next, string one round bead, one bicone, and another round bead and weave through the first bicone. Continue to stitch forward and exit from the newly added bicone. String one 11° and one 15° and weave through the corresponding middle 11° on the other triangle bezel. Then string one 15° and one 11°, weaving again through the second bicone in the link (figure 8, black path).

Continue to weave through the outside row of beads in the linking ring, stringing one 11° before and after each of the round beads. However, skip each of the 11° beads where you linked to the two existing triangular bezels—this will give the link sharper corners (figure 8, red path). Then weave a last time along the outside row and add four 15°s above each of the round beads (figure 8, green path).

Continue by connecting all the bezeled rose-colored chatons to the remaining corners of the square, and also repeat this step three more times to make links between each triangle bezel.

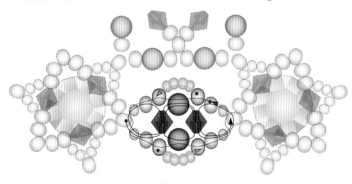

figure 8

9 To prepare for making and attaching the ring band, weave back to the base and exit from one of the 11° beads. Because the center of the ring band should be underneath a gold-colored chaton, start there from an 11° bead that follows one of the fire-polished beads to make an arc above the next fire-polished bead, as illustrated by the solid black path in figure 9. First string four 11°s, skip the fire-polished bead, and weave through the following 11° on the outside row of the base. Repeat two more times, then skip one fire-polished bead, weave through it, and make three more arcs above the following three fire-polished beads (figure 9).

figure 9

Finish

Follow the broken black line in figure 9 to start the ring band in double drop odd count peyote stitch (page 15) as follows: Exit from the third 11° bead in the first arc, string two 11°s (figure 9, red outlines), and weave through the two middle beads of the next arc. Continue by stringing two 11°s and weaving through the middle two beads in the next arc. Reverse direction for the next row.

Add three pairs of 11° beads (figure 9, green outlines) and continue to work in odd count peyote with a total of two pairs in the fourth and three pairs in the back row. The length of the band depends on the ring size, about 23 rows. End with a row that has two pairs of 11°s added, then zip the row to the beads on the other side of the ring. When securing the thread, weave several times through the beads of the starting and zipping rows to stabilize the band.

HOVERING CRYSTALS BRACELET

Embellishments can be sturdy enough to keep the space rigid between beads, even if those beads are far apart. This effect allows the bezeled chatons in this bracelet to hover above the base of round beads.

SUPPLIES

9 chatons, 8 mm (SS39), olive

28 round beads, 6 mm, green brown luster

36 fire-polished beads, 4 mm, lemon Picasso

72 bicones, 3 mm, crystal copper

6 g seed beads, 11°, gold color

7 g seed beads, 15°, metal iris gold

2 jump rings, 5 mm, 16 gauge, gold color

1 magnetic clasp

FireLine, 0.12 mm, 6 lb, smoke

Beading needle, size 12

Scissors

Chain-nose pliers

DIMENSIONS

7 inches (18 cm), not including clasp

1 String one fire-polished bead, one 11° bead, one round bead, and one 11°, then repeat this sequence three times. Then make a ring by weaving again through the fire-polished bead where you started. Weave a second time through the beads of the circle to secure the thread and exit in front of a round bead (figure 1).

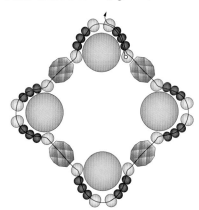

figure 1

2 String three 15° beads, two 11°s, and three 15°s, then skip the round bead to form an arc. Weave through the following 11°, fire-polished, and 11° beads. Repeat three times, then weave forward and exit from between the two 11° beads of the first arc (figure 2).

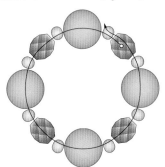

figure 2

3 String one 11°, then weave along the following beads of the row and through the first 11° bead of the next arc. Repeat three times to complete going around this row. At the end, exit from the first 11° added in this step (figure 3).

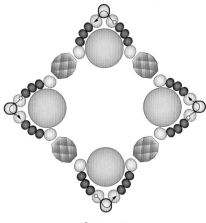

figure 3

4 String four 15°s, one 11°, and four 15°s, and weave through the middle 11° bead of the next arc.

Repeat three times. This pulls the arcs from the outside on top of the round beads, bringing a degree of tension into the beadwork. Weave a second time through the beads of the ring to secure it, then exit from an 11° added in this round (figure 4).

figure 4

5 String two 15°s, one 11°, and two 15°s, and weave through the next 11° of the previous step. Repeat three times to complete the row. Weave a second time through the beads of this row to secure the thread and exit from an 11° added in this step (figure 5).

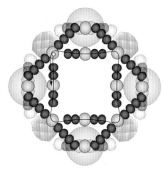

figure 5

6 String one 15°, one 11°, and one 15° and weave again through the 11° where you exited. Weave forward and exit from the next 11° added in the previous step. Repeat this step three times to complete going around. The four 11° beads added in this step are outlined in red in figure 6 and the following figures. Exit from the first 11° added in this step.

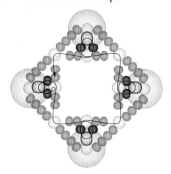

figure 6

7 The step up in the right angle weave unit will cause a change in beading direction.

String five 15°s and weave through the next 11° of the previous step. Repeat three times to complete going around. Loosen the thread and place a chaton in the cup, face up, then pull the thread and weave a second time through the beads of this ring. If the chaton is not secured properly, weave a third time through the beads of the ring, but skip the 11°s in the corners. Exit from one of the red-outlined 11°s in figure 7.

figure 7

8 String one 15°, one bicone, and one 15° and weave through the next 11° bead added in step 4, above a fire-polished bead. Continue by stringing one 15°, one bicone, and one 15°, then weave through the next 11° at the chaton bezel (figure 8, red outlines). Repeat three times to complete a circuit around the bezeled chaton.

figure 8

9 Starting again from one of the 11° beads outlined in faded red (figure 9), weave through the following 15° and bicone.

Next, string three 11°s, pushing them to form a picot, and weave through the following bicone and 15°. String one 15°, one 11°, and one 15°, skip the 11°, and weave through the following 15° and bicone. Repeat this step three times to complete going around. Weave back to the first row and exit from a round bead there to start the next unit (figure 9).

The first component is now complete.

figure 9

10 Starting from a round bead in the first component, string an 11° bead, a fire-polished bead, another 11°, and a round bead. Repeat two times and add an 11°, a fire-polished, and an 11°, then weave through the round bead where you started to form the base ring for the second component. Weave a second time through these beads, exiting from the last 11° strung in this new ring, in front of the round bead.

There is an 11° bead from the first unit on either side of the round bead. Weave through the closest of these 11°s and string an 11° (figure 10, top red outline), then weave again through the 11° where you exited; continue forward through the round bead and the first 11° strung for the second base ring. String an 11° bead (figure 10, bottom red outline) and weave through the adjacent 11°. Continue forward through the beads of the second base ring and exit from the second round bead, on the opposite side of the first component.

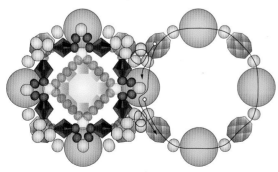

figure 10

Embellish this component by repeating steps 2 through 9. Make nine components attached to each other.

11 Make loops to add to the ends of the first and last components. Exit from an 11° at the beginning of the bracelet, optimally the 11° added in step 3 that is above one of the round beads. String five 11°s and weave again through the 11° where you started. Weave a second time through the beads of the loop and then a third time. Add a 15° in each gap between the second, third, fourth, and fifth 11° beads of the loop.

figure 11

Finish

Mount the clasp to the loops with jump rings.

HONEY HONEY BRACELET

This piece is made of six-sided components, some of which are embellished with a rivoli, and some not. One or two simple layers of embellishment turn a floppy base into a shaped, cuff-like bracelet.

SUPPLIES

21 rivolis, 8 mm, heliotrope

186 bicones, 3 mm, blue zircon 2AB

136 fire-polished beads, 4 mm, brown matte

2 g seed beads, 11°, metallic blue

7 g seed beads, 15°, light bronze

2 jump rings, 5 mm, 16 gauge, gold color

1 magnetic clasp

FireLine, 6 lb

Beading needle, size 12

Scissors

Chain-nose pliers

DIMENSIONS

7½ x ⅞ inches (19.1 x 2.2 cm), not including clasp

1 String one fire-polished bead and one 15° in sequence six times (12 beads on the needle). Make a ring by weaving again through the first bead strung, then weave a second time through the beads (figure 1).

figure 1

2 Continue making these six-sided rings to form a base, using figure 2 as a template. Start the next ring by exiting from a fire-polished bead. String one 15° and one fire-polished bead in sequence five times, ending with a 15°. Weave again through the fire-polished bead where you exited.

Following figure 2, attach a third ring to the first and the second. In addition to adding four new fire-polished beads, each one followed by a 15°, add a new 15° after the two fire-polished beads the new ring shares with the previous two.

Arrange these triangular-shaped rings so that they form a single unit next to a pair. Attach one more single unit to the pair, on the opposite side of the first single unit (refer to figure 2). Next, attach two ring units on the "free" side of the new single. Continue in this manner until the bracelet has the required length, starting and ending with a single unit. Here I used 11 singles and 10 pairs.

The numbers in figure 2 show the positions of the different embellishments as described in the following steps. Number 1 shows where embellishments with rivolis will be situated, and number 2 indicates the position of embellishments without a rivoli.

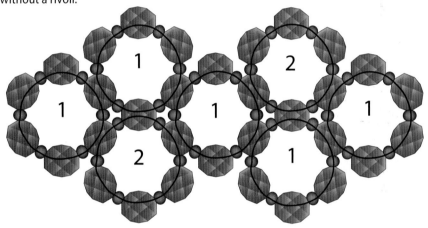

figure 2

3 Both embellishments start in the same way. For number 1, exit from a 15° bead. String two 15°s, one 11°, and two more 15°s, then skip the fire-polished bead and weave through the following 15° in this ring. Repeat five times to complete going around and exit from an 11° bead (figure 3).

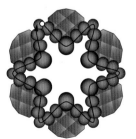

figure 3

4 String one bicone and weave through the following 11°. Repeat five times to complete going around. Loosen the thread and place the rivoli into the cup, front-side up. Pull the thread and weave another time through the beads to tighten it. Again, exit from a size 11° (figure 4).

figure 4

5 String four 15°s, skipping the bicone and weaving through the following 11°. Repeat five times to complete this round. Exit from the second 15° in the first group of four added in this step (figure 5).

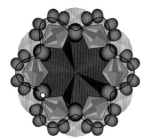

figure 5

6 String one 15° and weave through the following two 15°s, the next 11°, and the following two 15°s. Repeat five times to complete going around (figure 6). This completes embellishment number 1.

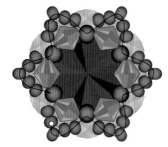

figure 6

Weave forward to the next ring on the base.

7 Repeat steps 3 and 4 to make embellishment number 2, but do not add a rivoli (figure 7). To stabilize the ring of bicones, weave another time through all six, skipping the 11° beads in between. This helps close that ring.

figure 7

Finish

Find a 15° bead between two fire-polished beads at each end of the bracelet. Make a loop there by stringing five 11°s and weaving another time through the 15° where you exited. Weave a second time through the beads of the loop, then a third time and add one 15° in each of the second, third, fourth, and fifth gaps between the 11° beads. Mount the clasp with the jump rings to the loops.

SUPPLIES

8 chatons, 8 mm, olivine

32 bicones, 3 mm, olivine satin

16 round beads, 3 mm, ancient rose

96 fire-polished beads, 4 mm, bronze

3 g double-hole beads (superduo or twin beads), chalk white Picasso

5 g seed beads, 11°, metallic ancient rose

4 g seed beads, 15°, light gold color

1 jump ring, 6 mm, brass color

1 silk ribbon, 18 to 36 inches (45 to 90 cm), depending on desired length

FireLine, 6 or 8 lb

Beading needle, size 12

Scissors

Flat-nose pliers

DIMENSIONS

2 x 2 x ½ inches (5.1 x 5.1 x 1.3 cm)

TILES ON A RING PENDANT

Circular rings need a sturdy construction so they don't morph into ovals. The easiest way for base rings to keep their shape is to attach chatons or rivolis.

Start with a wingspan of thread. You can add new thread as required when the original length is used up.

1 Make a row of 15 units in right angle weave. Start by stringing four fire-polished beads and make a circular pattern by weaving again through the first bead. String three more beads and weave again through the bead from which you exited (figure 1). Then stitch forward and exit from the second newly added bead. Repeat these steps until the 15 units are finished.

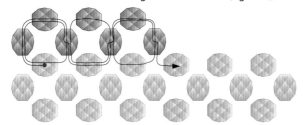

figure 1

Add a second row consisting of another 15 units, which includes the beads on the edge of the first row (figure 2).

figure 2

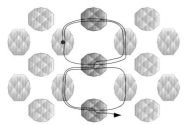

2 Form the strip you have created into a ring by using a 16th unit to attach the ends to each other (figure 3).

figure 3

3 Attach the upper and lower edges of the ring by using additional fire-polished beads as shown in figure 4. You now have a tube formed into a ring with three sides, one of which will be the inner-facing surface. Choose two adjacent rows and weave in a circular direction around the tube, going through all the beads, first in one row, then in the adjacent row (figure 5 and photo below). If required, weave a second time through so the beads are tight together.

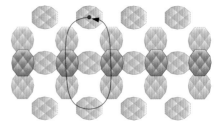

figure 4

figure 5

The following steps tell how to bezel the chatons. *Follow for every second unit of right angle weave.*

4 Continue weaving on one of the two outer sides on the tubed ring (this one is the front, and the third side will be the rear). There will be a total of 16 right angle weave units on this side. Weave through the four beads of one unit and add one 11° seed bead after each of the four fire-polished beads (figure 6). Exit from an 11° bead.

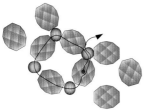

figure 6

5 String one 11° bead, one double-hole bead, and four 15° seed beads. Weave down through the second hole of the double-hole bead, string one 11°, and then weave through the adjacent 11° bead that you added in step 4. Repeat three times to complete the four sides as illustrated in figure 7, exiting after the second 15° bead of the four you strung at the beginning of this step.

figure 7

6 String one 11° bead and weave through the next two 15° beads (figure 8). String two 11°s and weave through the first two of the four 15°s that are above the next double-hole bead. Repeat another three times to complete the circuit. Exit from the first 11° bead added in this step.

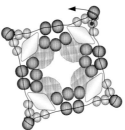

figure 8

7 String five 15°s and weave through the 11° above the next double-hole bead. Repeat another three times to complete this circuit, then loosen the thread and place the chaton into the cup you have created. Tighten the thread by pulling it and weaving a second time through the beads of this ring (figure 9). Exit from an 11° bead.

figure 9

Continue by stringing two 11° beads, one bicone, and two more 11°s, then weave through the following 11°. Repeat three times to complete the ring and exit before the first bicone added in this step (figure 10).

figure 10

8 Next, string four 15°s, skip the bicone, and weave through the following five 11°s. Repeat three more times to complete going around. Then, as illustrated by the black outlines in figure 11, add one 15° in the middle of each group of four 15°s just added.

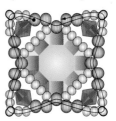

figure 11

9 Repeat steps 4 through 8 for every second right angle weave unit on one side of the ring. To stabilize the ring, weave through the 16 fire-polished beads on the outside edge, adding a pearl (or any other type of 3-mm round bead) after each of the fire-polished beads (figure 12).

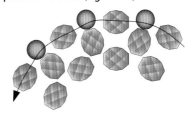

figure 12

10 Above one of the fire-polished beads on the outside edge, add an arc of five 11° beads. Make a loop with another five 11°s. Weave a second time through the beads of the loop and add a single 15° in each of the four gaps between the 11° beads (figure 13).

figure 13

Finish

Mount a jump ring in the loop and string the pendant onto a silk ribbon or chain.

SUPPLIES

32 bicones, 3 mm, padparadscha

32 bicones, 3 mm, sun

3 g seed beads, 15°, gold color

1 pair ear wires, gold

FireLine, 0.12 mm, 6 lb

Beading needle, size 12

Scissors

Chain nose-pliers

DIMENSIONS

2⁵⁄₈ x ¾ inches (6.7 x 1.9 cm)

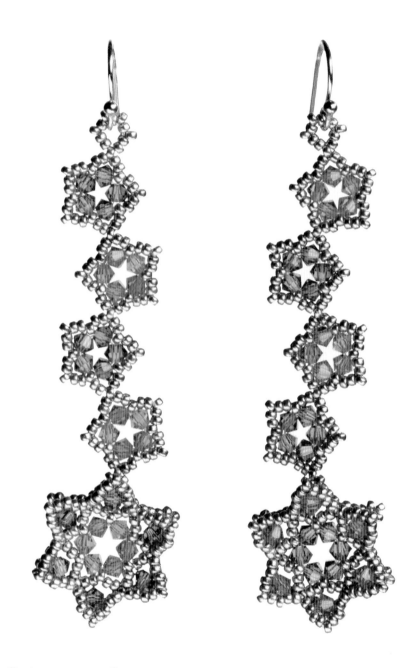

STARS WE ARE EARRINGS

Although these earrings appear to be made from separate components, each one is actually made in a single piece. Where using sun bicones in the first earring, use padparadscha in the second; and where using padparadscha in the first, use sun in the second.

1 Start by making a large beaded star. String six padparadscha bicones and make a ring by weaving again through the first bicone. Weave another two times through the entire ring.

2 Add one 15° seed bead in each gap between the bicones and exit from the first size 15° strung (figure 1).

figure 1

3 String four 15°s, skip the next bicone, and weave through the following 15° added in step 1. Repeat five times to complete going around (figure 2, solid black path) and exit between the second and third of the 15° beads strung first in this step.

4 String one 15° and weave through the following two 15°s. Skip the 15° in the gap between bicones and continue by weaving though the following two 15°s. Repeat five times (figure 2, broken black path). Exit from the first 15° added in this step.

figure 2

5 String seven 15°s and weave through the 15° bead in the middle of the arc above the next bicone. Repeat five times to complete going around and exit from the third bead of the first set of seven 15°s added in this step (figure 3).

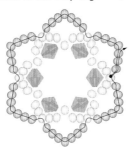

figure 3

6 String three 15°s, skip the fourth bead of the arc created in step 5, and weave through the following three 15°s. Skip the middle 15° (from step 4) in the arc above the bicone and weave through the following three 15°s. Repeat five times to complete going around. Form the groups of three 15°s into small picots—the middle bead should point out (figure 4).

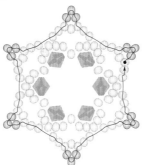

figure 4

7 Weave back to the beads added in step 4 (figure 5, red outlines) and exit from one of them. String two 15°s, one sun bicone, and two 15°s, and weave through the following 15° (strung in step 4). Repeat five times to complete the round and exit in front of the first bicone added in this round.

figure 5

8 String four 15° beads (figure 6, green outlines), skip the bicone, and weave through the following two 15°s. Skip the next 15° from step 4 (figure 6, red outlines) and weave through the following two 15°s. Repeat five times to complete the round and exit from between the second and third 15° beads added in this step (figure 6, solid black path).

9 String one 15° (figure 6, black outlines and broken black path) and weave through the following four 15°s, again skipping the 15° bead strung in step 4. Repeat five times to complete the round.

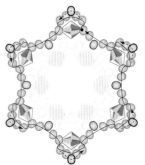

figure 6

10 To start making a small star, exit from the 15° of one tip created in step 6. String three 15° beads and five padparadscha bicones. Make a ring by weaving again through the first bicone. Make sure the ring is near the 15°s just strung, and that those are close to the large star (there should be no thread visible). Weave another time through the five bicones to secure the thread. Exit from the last bicone strung in this step (figure 7).

figure 7

11 Weave through the third 15° strung in the previous step, then through the following bicone. String one 15° bead and weave through the following bicone. Repeat three times to complete the round and exit from the 15° in front of the first bicone of the ring (figure 8).

figure 8

12 String four 15°s, skipping the bicone. Weave through the following 15°. Repeat three times, then string two 15°s and weave through the three 15°s strung in step 10 (figure 9, solid black path). Weave forward through the first two beads strung in this step and exit. Now add one 15° in the middle of each group of four 15°s (figure 9, broken black path and black outlines), forming a tip in four places, as illustrated.

figure 9

Continue to weave through the 15° bead from step 10 on the tip that "connects" the first and second stars. Then weave forward, skipping the following 15° beads between bicones.

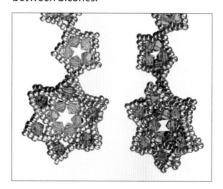

13 Now add three more small stars, making them as described in steps 10 through 12. Start from the tips, alternating bicone colors padparadscha and sun

as illustrated figure 10. Counting clockwise from the previous connecting point, add the third star from the second tip and the fourth star from the third tip.

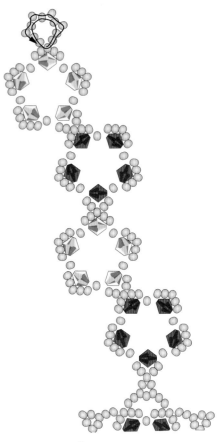

figure 10

14 At the end, make a loop. Starting from the 15° of one tip, string seven 15° beads. Weave again through the 15° where you started. Then weave again through the beads of the loop and add one 15° bead in the third, fourth, fifth, and sixth gaps between the beads of the loop.

Finish

Make a second earring in the same way, but exchange the colors and attach the small stars so that the second one is the mirror image of the first. Therefore, attach the third star on the third tip and the fourth star on the second tip.

Mount the earrings with their loops to the ear wires.

V: Go Dimensional

Dimensional beadwork, such as beaded beads or beaded spheres, is for sure my (not so) secret love. Created either from single components that are connected later, or based on a lattice that becomes more sturdy with added layers, these are like little treasures that literally grow in your hand.

SUPPLIES

2 rivolis, 18 mm*, vitrail light

6 chatons, 8 mm (SS39), amethyst color

36 bicones, 3 mm, amethyst color

4 g seed beads, 11°, metallic red gold color

1 g seed beads, 15°, metallic yellow gold color

1 jump ring, 6 mm, gold color

FireLine, 6 or 8 lb

Beading needle, size 12

Scissors

Chain-nose pliers

* Use 16 mm if you tend to have a high tension.

DIMENSIONS

1¼ x 9/16 inches (3.2 x 1.4 cm)

SPARKLELICIOUS PENDANT

With chatons and rivolis on all sides, structures like this are so sturdy you can let loose in the beginning and not raise your tension until the last steps.

1 Cut one and a half wingspans of thread. You will make a base for this pendant that consists of right angle weave units that alternate between rectangular and square shapes. Follow along with figure 1.

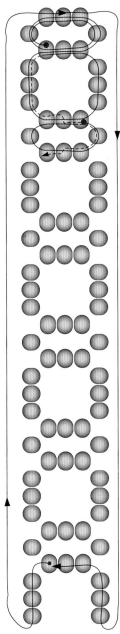

figure 1

String eight 11° seed beads and weave a second time through all of them to secure the thread, forming a thin, rectangular ring. Exit from the last bead and string nine 11° seed beads, then weave through the last three beads of the first rectangular unit. Stitch forward through the next six beads and exit, forming a square-shaped unit adjacent to the original rectangular unit.

String five 11°s and weave through the last three beads of the previous (square) unit. Stitch forward through the next four beads to form a second rectangular unit that is adjacent to the square unit.

Continue in this manner to alternate rectangular and square units to make a base strip. After finishing the sixth rectangle, connect the ends of the base strip as follows: String three 11° seed beads, then weave through the three seed beads on the other end of the strip. String three more 11° seed beads and weave through the last three beads of the sixth rectangle to form the base into a ring.

2 Weave through the beads along the edge of the base ring to exit after a group of three beads from a square unit. String one 11° seed bead and weave through the next bead at the top of the next rectangular unit on the base. Then string three 11° seed beads and weave again through the original top bead that you just exited. This creates a new right angle weave unit above the original top bead.

Now string one 11° seed bead and weave through the next group of three seed beads. Repeat until you have created six right angle weave units all the way around one edge of the ring. Then repeat on the other edge of the ring (figure 2).

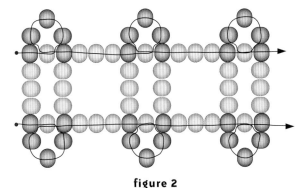

figure 2

3 In the previous step, you not only created a number of right angle weave units, but you also filled the four corners of each square in the base with one 11° seed bead. Exit from one of these corner beads and string three 11° seed beads, weaving again through the corner bead from which you just exited. Weave through beads to exit from the 11° in the next corner of this square. Repeat, making similar right angle weave units at the other three corners of the square (figure 3).

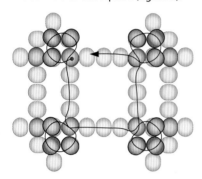

figure 3

4 Follow figure 4 to create a cup on one of the square base units into which you will place a chaton. For reference, the faded beads in figure 4 show the second of three size 11°s added in the previous step.

Exit from the second of the three consecutive 11° beads strung in one of the corners in step 3 (red dot in figure 4). String one 11° bead, one bicone, and another 11°, and weave through the second of the three beads on the next right angle weave unit from step 3. Repeat another three times to complete going around.

Loosen the thread and put a chaton into the cup. Pull the thread and weave a second time through the beads of the row. Exit in front of a bicone.

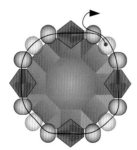

figure 4

5 String four 15° seed beads and skip the bicone to weave through the next three 11° seed beads. Repeat three more times, working your way around the chaton (figure 5, black path). Weave through the first two 15°s strung in this step.

Then string one 11° seed bead and weave through the following seven beads (two 15°s, three 11°s, and two 15°s). Repeat, adding one 11° in the other three corners (figure 5, red path).

figure 5

6 Repeat steps 3, 4, and 5 to add bezeled chatons to the other five square units of the base. Because you are working on a ring, the units will share beads and you won't have to add new beads where they join. Instead, weave through the 11° that is present on the previous unit (figure 6). Be aware that the last (sixth) unit will be attached to the previous ones on both sides.

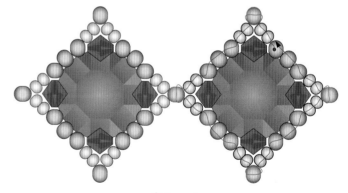

figure 6

7 Exit from the middle of three consecutive 11° seed beads to make one of the right angle weave units in step 2 (figure 7, red outlines). String one 15°, one 11°, one bicone, one 11°, and one 15°, then weave through the 11° in the middle of the following right angle weave unit on this edge of the base. Repeat five times to work around the ring. Loosen the thread and put a rivoli in the cup. Pull the thread and weave a second time through the newly added beads of the ring to secure the thread and hold the tension. Exit from the 11° bead from which you first exited to start this step.

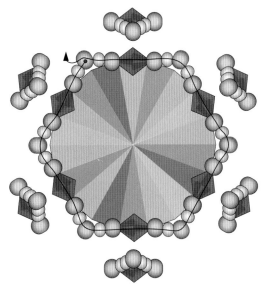

figure 7

8 String one 11° and two 15° seed beads and weave through the 11° on the tip of the bezeled chaton. String two 15°s and one 11° and weave through the 11° of the next right angle weave unit you made in step 2.

figure 8

Repeat this procedure five times to complete the ring, as illustrated by the black path and black bead outlines in figure 8.

Weave through and exit in front of the next unit of right angle weave from step 2. Following the red path in figure 8, string one 15°, one 11°, and one 15°. Skip the following 11° in the unit and weave through the next seven beads—one 11°, two 15°s, one 11°, two 15°s, and one 11°. Push the three added beads (figure 8, red outlines) into a picot so that the middle bead points out of the group.

Repeat this procedure five times to place a total of six picots around the ring.

9 Go to the other side of the base and repeat steps 7 and 8. Then make a loop starting from any 11° seed bead found between two adjacent bezeled chatons. To do so, exit from this 11° bead, string five 11° beads, and weave again through the 11° bead from which you exited. Weave a second time through the beads of the loop to hold the tension. Finally, add a 15° bead in each of the four gaps of the loop.

Finish

Mount a jump ring into the loop and string the pendant on a silk ribbon or chain.

Variation

If desired, you could make a second loop on the opposite side of this piece and integrate the pendant into a chain, or even make several pendants to connect to a chain. Use rivolis of different colors in the pendant and see how the sparkle changes whenever the pendant turns around. Due to the shape of this pendant, all facets will be visible when mounted as described here.

SUPPLIES

4 rivolis, 8 mm (SS39), heliotrope

24 tourmaline bicones, 3 mm, green

12 fire-polished beads, 4 mm,
iris green

12 round beads, 3 mm, lavender

2 g seed beads 11°, metal iris gold

2 g seed beads 15°, gold color

2 ear wires, gold color

FireLine, 6 lb

Beading needle, size 12

Scissors

Chain-nose pliers

DIMENSIONS

2 x ¾ inches (5.1 x 1.9 cm)

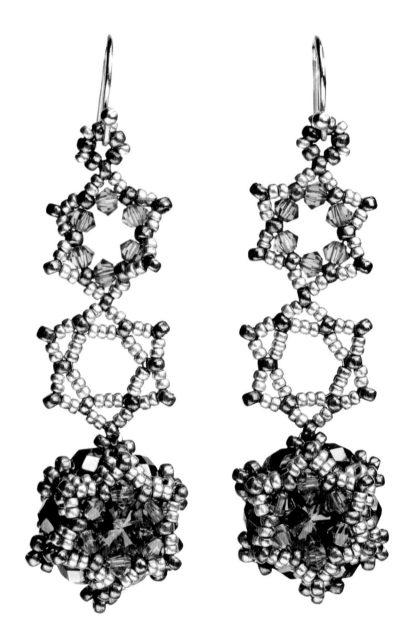

JERUSALEM EARRINGS

**Dimensional structures don't need to be large—they can be made
small enough to craft a pair of delicate earrings.**

1 String one fire-polished bead and one 11° seed bead and repeat five times. Weave again through the entire ring of 12 beads to secure the thread, exiting from the first fire-polished bead (figure 1).

figure 1

2 To make the front bezel, string one 15° seed bead, one 11°, and another 15°, then weave through the following fire-polished bead. Repeat five times to complete going around and exit from the first 11° bead added in this step (figure 2).

figure 2

3 String two 15°s, one 11°, and two 15°s, skip the following three beads (a 15°, a fire-polished bead, and a 15°), and weave through the following 11° from step 2. Repeat five times to complete the round and exit from the first 11° added in this step (figure 3).

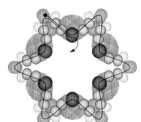

figure 3

4 String one 15°, one 11°, and one 15°, then weave again through the bead where you exited step 3. This produces a right angle weave unit on top of this 11° bead. Weave forward along the following five beads of the previous round (two 15°s, one 11°, and two 15°s) and into the following 11°. Repeat this weaving pattern five times to complete the round. Exit from the first 11° added in this round. Your beading direction will change due to the step up in a right angle weave unit (figure 4).

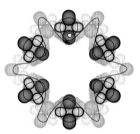

figure 4

5 String one bicone and weave through the 11° in the middle of the next right angle weave unit (this is the 11° added in the previous step). Repeat five times to complete the round. Loosen the thread and put a rivoli into the cup, front-side up. Pull the thread and weave a second time through the beads to secure the thread. Exit from an 11° (figure 5).

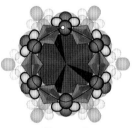

figure 5

6 String two 15°s, one 11°, and two more 15°, skip the bicone, and weave through the following 11° bead. Repeat five times to complete going around (figure 6). If you want to enhance the points of the star, weave another time through the beads added in this step, but this time skip the 11° beads that form the six tips.

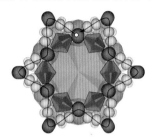

figure 6

7 To make the rear bezel, weave back to the original ring of 12 beads strung in step 1. Repeat steps 2 through 4 on the other side of the ring.

8 After exiting from the indicated 11° bead, string one 3-mm round bead and weave through the 11° in the middle of the next right angle weave unit (this is the 11° added in the previous step). Repeat five times to complete going around. Loosen the thread and put a rivoli into the cup, front-side up. Pull the thread and weave a second time through the beads to secure it. Then repeat step 6 before exiting from an 11° (figure 7).

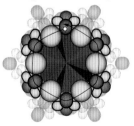

figure 7

Weave back to the beads of the first round and exit from a fire-polished bead.

9 String three 11°s and weave through the following fire-polished bead. Form a picot with these beads, which will be between the ones you made at the beginning of the front and rear bezels. Repeat five times as illustrated in figure 8, and then exit from a middle 11° bead of a picot created in this step.

figure 8

10 The next star-shaped element is beaded from the outside to the inside.

Following the black path in figure 9, string two 15°s and one 11°, then repeat 10 times. Then string two more 15°s (this makes a total of 35 beads). Weave again through the 11° from step 9 where you started. Weave through the following five beads (two 15°s, one 11°, and two 15°s), then skip the following 11°. Repeat this weaving pattern five times, which produces six star points, or tips.

figure 9

Exit from the first 11° added in this step and, following the red path in figure 9, string three 15°s. Skip the following five beads (again, two 15°s, one 11°, and two 15°s) and weave through the next 11°. Repeat five times to complete the inner hexagon of the star. Weave another time through the beads of this inner part and, if possible, also through the beads of the outer perimeter (again skipping the 11° beads that form the six tips of the star).

11 Starting from the 11° that is directly opposite the bezeled rivoli, make another star. Repeat the pattern in the first part of step 10 to form the outside shape, stringing the 35 beads of the outline. Weave again through the beads, but skip the 11° bead at each point. For the inner element, replace each set of three 15° beads with a 3-mm bicone (six total). Weave another time through the outside perimeter of the star to secure it (figure 10).

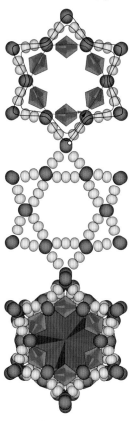

figure 10

12 Finally, make a loop starting from the 11° bead on top of the second star. String five 11°s and weave again through all the beads of the loop. Finally, add one 15° in the second, third, fourth, and fifth gaps between the 11°s (figure 11).

figure 11

Finish

Make a second earring in the same way. Mount the ear wires to the loops on top of the earrings.

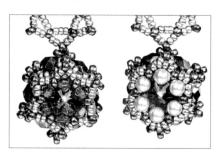

The front and the back of the primary elements.

SUPPLIES

12 chatons, 8 mm (SS39), Sahara blue

60 bicones, 3 mm, green

30 fire-polished beads, 4 mm, lime green

4 g drop beads, 3.4 mm, green lime lined

3 g seed beads, 15°, mint green

1 jump ring, 5 mm, 16 gauge, gold color

FireLine, 6 lb

Beading needle, size 12

Scissors

Chain-nose pliers

DIMENSIONS

1⅛ inches (2.9 cm) in diameter

BUBBLE BALL PENDANT

This sphere is made from 12 equal components, each based on a ring of five fire-polished beads. Geometrically, this kind of 12-surfaced polyhedron is known as a dodecahedron. If you search "platonic bodies" on the Internet, you will find a multitude of geometric shapes, and all of them can be produced with beads!

1 String five consecutive pairs of one fire-polished bead and one 15° seed bead for a total of 10 beads onto the needle. Make a ring by weaving again through the first bead. Weave a second time through the beads of the circle to secure the thread and exit from a 15° in the end (figure 1).

figure 1

2 String three 15°s, one drop bead, and three more 15°s. Skip the fire-polished bead and weave through the following 15°. Repeat four times to complete going around the ring and exit from a drop bead (figure 2).

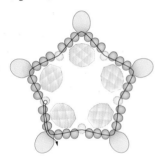

figure 2

3 String one bicone and weave through the following drop bead. Repeat four times to complete going around. Loosen the thread and put the chaton, front-side up, into the cup (figure 3). Pull the thread and weave another time through the beads of the round to create stronger tension. Exit from a drop bead.

figure 3

4 String four 15° beads, skip the bicone, and weave through the following drop bead. Repeat four times to finish going around and completing the first component. Weave back to the first ring made in step 1 and exit from a fire-polished bead (figure 4).

figure 4

5 Make more base rings as in step 1, always starting from the fire-polished bead of the previous one.

For the second ring, string four paired sets in sequence, consisting of one 15° and one fire-polished bead, then add one more 15° (five 15°s and four fire-polished beads on the needle, figure 5). Make a ring by weaving again through the fire-polished bead where you exited and work the embellishments.

Add the component embellishments described in steps 2 through 4 to each base ring as you complete it. The single components are much easier to identify once their shape is sturdy due to the bezeled chaton.

figure 5

6 To make the third base ring, include one fire-polished bead from the first circle and one from the second circle, adding a 15° between them, as illustrated in figure 6. String three sequential pairs of beads consisting of one 15° followed by a fire-polished bead. Embellish.

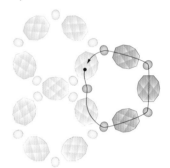

figure 6

7 Work your way around the base row of your first circle until it is surrounded by five other units. The last unit will be attached to the first, fifth, and second units you created. By this time you will be adding only two new fire-polished beads. The beadwork forms a cup at this point, which is the first half of a beaded ball (figure 7).

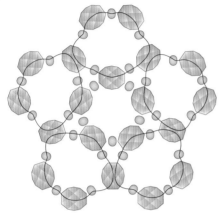

figure 7

8 Refer to figure 8 when making the first component of the second half, which shows how to include a fire-polished bead from each of two adjacent components of the first half. Note that you still have to add one 15° between all of the fire-polished beads of your base circles and work the embellishment for each component as soon as its base circle is finished.

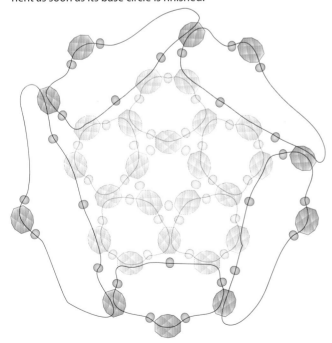

figure 8

When you have added five components along the rim of the first half, the sphere is almost complete.

9 Complete the last ring by adding 15° beads where needed between the five fire-polished beads, then embellish (figure 9).

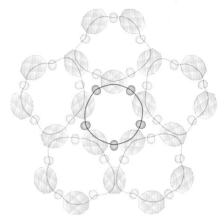

figure 9

Finish

The easiest way to mount this pendant is to create a link between the drop beads of two adjacent components. Exit from one drop bead, string two 15°s, and weave through the drop bead of the adjacent unit. String two more 15°s and weave again through the drop bead where you started. Weave as often as you can through the beads of this circle, then secure the thread and cut it. Mount the jump ring under this little bridge.

SUPPLIES

75 fire-polished beads, 4 mm, purple iris

120 round beads, 3 mm, lavender

60 bicones, 3 mm, light amethyst 2AB

4 g seed beads, 11°, metallic eggplant

4 g seed beads, 15°, purple

15 g seed beads, 15°, metallic olive

FireLine, 6 lb

Beading needle, size 12

Scissors

DIMENSIONS

1½ inches (3.8 cm) in diameter

SPARKLING FOOTBALL PENDANT

Footballs, or soccer balls in the U.S., are often made with black pentagon-shaped pieces of leather surrounded by white, hexagon-shaped pieces. If you have no experience in beading spheres, I suggest you try the Bubble Ball first (see pages 113-115).

The hexagonal unit in this piece is embellished with round beads; the pentagonal shape is embellished with bicones. There is a template at the end of these steps to show how the units are arranged.

1 Start with a pentagonal shape. String one fire-polished bead and one purple 15° in sequence five times. Make a ring by weaving again through the first bead and then through all beads. Exit from a 15° (figure 1).

figure 1

2 String two purple 15°s, one 11° bead, and two purple 15°s. Then skip the fire-polished bead and weave through the next 15°. Repeat four times, creating small arcs, and exit from the 11° in the middle of the first arc (figure 2).

figure 2

3 String one bicone and weave through the following 11°. Repeat four times to complete going around. Weave a second time through the beads of this step to secure the thread and exit from an 11° (figure 3).

figure 3

4 String four green 15°s, skip the bicone, and weave through the following 11°. Repeat four times to complete going around (figure 4, black path). Exit from the second of the first four 15°s in this step and string another green 15°. Weave through the following two 15°s, one 11°, and two 15°s. Repeat the step four times to complete the round (figure 4, red path).

figure 4

5 Weave back to the base of the pentagon and exit from a fire-polished bead. String one purple 15° and one fire-polished bead in sequence five times. This is a base ring for a hexagon. Continue by stringing one more purple 15° and weave again through the fire-polished bead of the pentagonal base where you exited (figure 5).

Whenever you make an additional base ring, whether pentagon or hexagon, weave through the fire-polished beads of the adjacent ring, and always add a purple 15° bead in between each fire-polished bead—those 15°s are not shared by adjacent units!

figure 5

6 The embellishment for the hexagon begins in the same way as the pentagon. Exiting from a purple 15° of the base ring, string two purple 15°s, one 11°, and two more purple 15°s. Skip the fire-polished bead and weave through the following 15°. Repeat five times to complete going around. Exit from an 11° bead (figure 6).

figure 6

7 String one round bead and weave through the following 11°. Repeat five times to complete the round. Then weave another time through the round beads only, skipping the 11°s in between. Weave as often as needed through the beads to make the construction sturdier (figure 7).

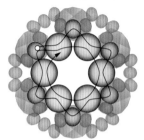

figure 7

8 Start building the ball by surrounding the first pentagonal unit (number 1 in figure 8) with five hexagonal units (numbers 2 through 6 in figure 8). Embellish each unit, pentagonal or hexagonal, as soon as you finish it.

Add unit 2 to unit 1 as described in step 5. Unit 3 is adjacent to both units 1 and 2. Weave through the fire-polished bead in unit 2 that is adjacent to unit 3, then string one purple 15° and one fire-polished bead in sequence four times. Add another purple 15°, then weave through the adjacent fire-polished bead of unit 1 and string one more purple 15° before weaving again through the fire-polished bead of unit 2. Add units 4 and 5 in a similar manner.

Note in figure 8 that unit 6 is adjacent to units 1, 2, and 5. Consequently, add only three new fire-polished beads, but six new purple 15°s.

After surrounding unit 1 with five hexagonal units, add pentagonal units as shown by the green pattern in figure 8 (units 7, 8, 9, 10, and 11). Once this is accomplished, add five hexagonal units between them (purple pattern, units 12, 13, 14, 15, and 16 in figure 8).

A cup is forming at this point and the ball is half finished. Continue the second half by adding hexagons, first attached to units 12, 7, and 13, and then a second attached to units 13, 8, and 14, and so on. After that, fill the gaps between those five added hexagonal units with pentagons.

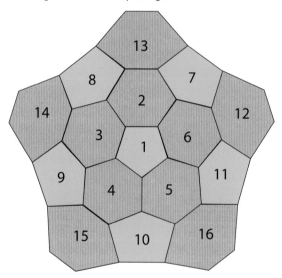

figure 8

9 To complete the ball, add a final ring of hexagonal units (like numbers 2 through 6) and one last pentagon.

Finish

String the football onto a silk ribbon and wear as a pendant.

Variation

One variation might include adding a selection of 8-mm rivolis into the hexagons. See also the rivoli bezels in the Honey Honey Bracelet on page 98.

SUPPLIES

4 chatons, 8 mm (SS39), copper

32 bicones, 3 mm, crystal copper

14 round beads, 8 mm, ancient green

2 g drop beads, 3.4 mm, crystal copper

1 g seed beads, 11°, gold color

2 g seed beads, 15°, light bronze

1 eye pin, 6 cm, 18 gauge, copper

1 copper charm

1 jump ring, 5 mm, 16 gauge, copper

FireLine, 6 lb

Beading needle, size 12

Scissors

Chain-nose pliers

Round nose-pliers

DIMENSIONS

1¾ x 1 inches (4.4 x 2.5 cm)

ROUND CUBE PENDANT

This piece is based on a unit of cubic right angle weave made from 8-mm round beads. It ultimately appears as a round sphere due to the embellishments.

1 String four round beads and make a square by weaving again through the first bead. Weave another time through all four beads. This is the base of the cube (figure 1).

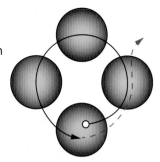

figure 1

2 String three round beads and weave again through the bead where you exited. Then weave forward into the next bead of the base (figure 2, broken red path). The first side of your cube is finished.

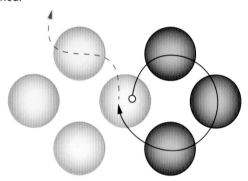

figure 2

3 Following the solid black path in figure 3, string two round beads and weave through the round bead of the previous unit and the round bead of the base where you exited. Then weave forward into the next round bead of the base (figure 3, broken red path). The second side is finished.

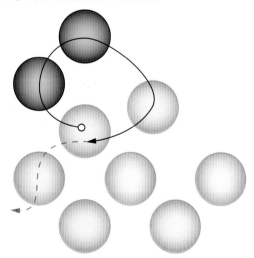

figure 3

4 String two round beads and weave through the round bead of the previous unit and the round bead of the base, where you exited (figure 4, solid black path). Then weave forward into the next round bead of the base and the round bead of the first

side of the cube (figure 4, broken red path). The third side is finished, and the walls are folding up.

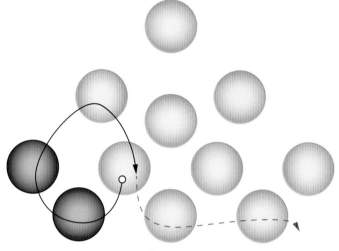

figure 4

5 String one round bead and weave through the next round bead of the previous unit (figure 5, solid black path) . The fourth side is finished.

Secure the cube by weaving forward in a square through the beads of this fourth unit and exit from the bead on the top—the last bead added (figure 5, broken red path). Starting from this bead, weave along the four beads on top of the four sides (figure 5, solid red path). This is the top, or lid, of the cube.

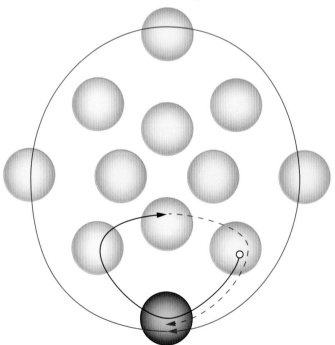

figure 5

Steps 6 through 10 illustrate the embellishment work for the four sides of the cube. The base and the lid are embellished in a different way (steps 6, 7, and 12).

6 Weave along the four round beads of one side and add a drop bead between each (figure 6).

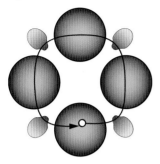

figure 6

7 Exit from a drop bead. String four 15° beads, one 11° bead, and four more 15°s, then skip the round bead and weave through the following drop bead. Repeat three times to complete the ring. Exit from an 11° bead (figure 7).

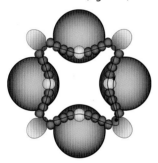

figure 7

8 String four 15°s and weave through the 11° that is in the next arc strung in step 7. Repeat three times to complete going around. Loosen the thread and place a chaton into the cup, front-side up (figure 8).

figure 8

Weave once more through the beads of the row and tighten the thread. Exit from an 11°.

9 String one bicone, one 11°, and one bicone, then weave through the next 11° in the circle. Repeat three times to complete the round. Exit after the first bicone added in this step (figure 9).

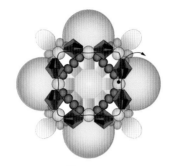

figure 9

10 String one 15°, one 11°, and one 15°, skip the 11° in the corner, and weave through the following three beads (bicone, 11°, and bicone). Repeat three times to complete this round (figure 10). The embellishment is finished.

Repeat steps 6 through 10 on the other three sides of the cube.

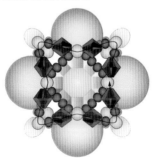

figure 10

11 Repeat steps 6 and 7 to begin the embellishment for the top and bottom of the cube.

12 Exit from the 11° bead in one of the arcs. String three 15° beads and weave through the 11° of the following arc. Repeat three times to complete the round (figure 11). Then, skipping the 11° beads in the corners, weave another time through the 15° beads.

Repeat this on the other end of the cube.

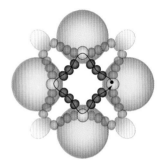

figure 11

Finish

String one 8-mm round bead on the eye pin and then run the pin all the way through the center of the cube. String one more round bead.

Make a loop in the top of the eye pin and mount it to the jump ring. On the other end, mount the charm pendant to the loop of the eye pin.

For a better security, I prefer making a double loop on top of the pin. Using the round-nose pliers, take a longer piece of wire on the end of the head pin and roll it in twice.

GALLERY

1 MIRIAM SHIMON
Chain of Emotion, 2013
40 x 18 x 14 cm
Seed beads, crystals, pearls; soutache
embroidery, bead embroidery
Photo by artist

2 CYNTHIA NEWCOMER DANIEL
Whimisical Lace, 2013
Focal section: 6 x 5 cm; overall length: 18 cm
Seed beads; modified right-angle weave,
right-angle weave, netting, square stitch
Photo by artist

3 PEGGY HEIDRICH
Estelle, 2013
4.5 x 1 cm
Round beads, seed beads, bicone beads,
rivoli beads; right-angle weave, peyote
stitch
Photo by artist

4 PEGGY HEIDRICH
Sharona, 2013
4.5 x 1 cm
Seed beads, fire-polished beads, rivoli
beads, bicone beads, spikes, round beads
Photo by artist

5 CINDY HOLSCLAW
*Serotonin and Dopamine
Necklace,* 2013
40 x 2 x 0.2 cm
Seed beads; infinity weave, netting
Photo by artist

1

2

3

4

5

1 MIRIAM SHIMON
Eden, 2013
38 x 18 x 15 cm
Seed beads, crystals, pearls; soutache embroidery,
bead embroidery
Photo by artist

2 ERIKA PFISTER
Lucky Star, 2013
20 x 2.5 x 1 cm
Seed beads, drops, rivoli beads, bicone beads;
peyote stitch, herringbone stitch
Photo by artist

3 ÈVA DOBOS
Foina, 2013
10 cm in diameter
Pearls, fire-polished beads, seed beads; embel-
lished, right-angle weave
Photo by Sándor Bodogán

4 CINDY HOLSCLAW
Tequila Earrings, 2013
Each: 5 x 3 x 3 cm
Photo by artist

5 CYNTHIA NEWCOMER DANIEL
Desert Rose, 2013
Focal section: 5 x 15 cm; overall length: 48 cm
Seed beads, Swarovski pearls; modified right-angle
weave, right-angle weave, herringbone stitch,
peyote stitch, fringing, netting, square stitch
Photo by artist

2

3

4

5

1 NANCY DALE
Turtle Cove Beaded Sculpture, 2013
29 cm in diameter
Seed beads, Swarovski crystal, freshwater
pearls, glass, turquoise, found rocks; freeform
peyote stitch, right-angle weave, fringing
Beaded fish based on the Fancy Fish Friends
by Karen Williams
Photo by Sherwood Lake Photography

2 CINDY HOLSCLAW
Red Wine Chemistry Necklace, 2013
43 x 4 x 3 cm
Seed beads, crystals; molecule stitch
Photo by artist

Photo by Beate Knappe

About the Author

Sabine Lippert lives in Germany and has loved crafting and needlework since she was a child. As an adult, Sabine pursued a career as a physician, working in private practice, when, in 2006, she stumbled across a favorite little bead shop in her hometown of Bonn. Since then her life has changed completely!

After publishing her first patterns in a friend's online shop and teaching workshops in that local bead store, Sabine's first book, *Das Perlenkochbuch*, was published in Germany in 2009. Her second book, *Sabine Lippert's Beaded Fantasies*, was published in English by Lark Books in 2012.

Sabine currently has her own webshop for beading patterns and kits and is teaching her designs worldwide (trytobead.com). In 2014 she finally quit her job as a physician and has taken up the world of beading as the major occupation in her life. She still resides in Bonn with her beloved little dog, Pia, and her beads.

Acknowledgments

To my friends and family who accept me as I am, which is sometimes funny, sometimes grumpy. To my mother who supported me in dedicating my life to my dreams. To my father who was in this world for way too short of a time.

To my sister, who is my best companion in the world.

To Nathalie Mornu and Kevin Kopp at Lark Jewelry and Beading; the first who acquired this book project, and the second who did a great job with the copyedit and had a lot of patience with me.

To Claudia Schumann, who made the technical edit and who also gave me the chance of my life by publishing my first book.

To Petra Tismer, for selling me my first beads and giving me the opportunity to teach my first workshops.

And last but not least, to all the beaders in the world, who support me and give me feedback for my work.

INDEX